AND THE PASSENGER
WAS DEATH

The Drama and Trauma
of Losing a Child

Douglas Daher

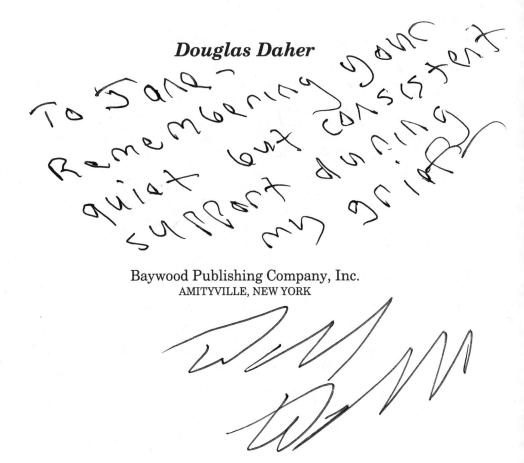

To Jane -
Remembering your
quiet but consistent
support during
my grief

Baywood Publishing Company, Inc.
AMITYVILLE, NEW YORK

Baywood Publishing Company, Inc.
26 Austin Avenue
Amityville, NY 11701
(800) 638-7819
E-mail: baywood@baywood.com
Web site: baywood.com

Library of Congress Catalog Number: 2003043726
ISBN: 0-89503-244-9 (paper)

Library of Congress Cataloging-in-Publication Data

Daher, Douglas, 1949-
     And the passenger was death : the drama and trauma of losing a child / Douglas Daher.
          p. cm.
     Includes bibliographical references and index.
     ISBN 0-89503-244-9 (pbk. : alk. paper)
     1. Grief. 2. Bereavement--Psychological aspects. 3. Children--Death--Psychological aspects. 4. Loss (Psychology) I. Title.

     BF575.G7D34 2003
     155.9'37--dc21

                                                                          2003043726

Cover photo by Allen Sciutto
Cover design consultation and assistance by Casey Alt

Royalties will be donated to the Andrew Daher Fellowship at the Haas Center for Public Service, Stanford University.

Contents

Dedication.   v

Acknowledgments.   vii

Epigraph   ix

Introduction   1

ACT I—First Week   3
  The Delivery.   3
  The Ride   5
  The Confusion.   6
  The Planning   8
  The First Night   11
  The Company   12
  The Detective   14
  The Visit   15
  The Dream.   19
  The Informing.   20
  The Wake   24
  The Funeral   28
  The Circle   34

ACT II—Players 39
   Protection 40
   Matching Stars 41
   Cleared-Eyed 42
   Cracking Glass. 43

ACT III—Inside 45
   The Crying. 45
   The Despair 47
   The Anger 52
   The Longing 54
   The Remembering. 57
   The Forgetting 60
   The Loss 62
   The Attachment 64

ACT IV—Systems 69
   The Bank 70
   The Worker's Compensation 72
   The Insurance 74
   The Preamble 77
   The Lawsuit 78

ACT V—Rituals 87
   Tree Planting 87
   Ashes. 89
   Second Anniversary 94

ACT VI—Healing 99
   Relationships 102
   Conclusion 105
   Postscript 106

Resources 109

References 111

Index. 113

About the Author 118

Dedication

to Carrie,
no better fellow traveler
down this very sad path
than you

Acknowledgments

Jeffrey Moulton Benevedes, for his listening in the early stages of this writing in monkish silence, as agreed.

Carole Pertofski and Tom Harshman who provided essential support and commentary as I drafted.

Gene and Nancy Knott, for passing this manuscript on to Dr. John Morgan at Baywood and affirming its relevance in their remembrance of their son Gavin.

The Big Three, Susan Kaplan, Casey Alt, and Jeff Janger, for hours upon hours of insightful critiques of my writing, fearless challenges when I was murky, and unending encouragement.

Jimmy Canton and Andy Canale, for such depth of empathy when responding to their readings that there was never an option but to bring this book to completion.

To the other actors in this drama of losing Andy, I stand in awe of your endurance and strength. I fully acknowledge that your experiences and remembrances may differ from mine, such is our nature.

Lastly, my daughter, Carolyn Marie Daher, who was willing to symbolically relive the loss of her brother through her several readings of and responses to this writing in order to enhance her father's accuracy and balance in the telling of this story.

Epigraph

Tonight all the hells of young grief have opened again; the mad words, the bitter resentment, the fluttering in the stomach, the nightmare unreality, the wallowed-in tears. For in grief nothing 'stays put.' One keeps on emerging from a phase, but it always recurs. Round and round. Everything repeats. Am I going in circles, or dare I hope I am on a spiral?

But if a spiral, am I going up or down?

C. S. Lewis
A Grief Observed

Introduction

This book is not a memoir of my son, Andrew Jacob Daher. Nor is this book very much about who I am, as his father. Rather, these reflections are about a father in grief and struggling to make sense of the tragic death of his son. I first and foremost wanted to share my stories and whatever insights I have rendered from them with others who have experienced sudden (or even not so sudden) loss of loved ones, and in particular, fathers and mothers whose children have died. In observing my own capacities in grief, or more to the point, lack of capacity, I was aware that I could not read for long periods of time. Books on death and grief that friends steered me toward were often too dense and required too much concentration. In my constant pain, focused and consistent attentiveness was not often an option. What I found I could sustain was reading short passages by authors who had experienced grief, telling about what happened to them and how they were coping.

Based on knowledge that with grief we manage the best we can, I have narrated my story in themes that are only several pages long, with short reflections along the way. I am keenly aware that this is my story, and that the pain readers face is unique to them and will not necessarily be soothed by reading about my loss and coping. If, however, you recognize spoken words, gestures, and turns of events within this two-year drama that speak to your own tragedies, and you feel less alone, then I am also less alone. Grief is initiation into a privileged *club* in which none of us who belong would have chosen membership. Nonetheless, once we are inducted, often those outside cannot comprehend the dues we have paid.

ACT I
First Week

THE DELIVERY

Dreaded news arrives by means that become instantly insignificant once the delivery is completed. In past decades, telegraphs, the letter from the War Department, the neighbor with the only phone in rural farmlands walking upon the stone path to the screen door, or the official telephone call from the local police were the scripts. In my case, it was a phone call recorded on an answering machine message at four in the morning. In responding to the message, I heard my son's mother, sobbing, say that Andy, our only son, is dead.

I am a figure of glass on a glass mantel, attached to a glass wall, in a glass house, located within a glass community, a part of a glass country, which is located on glass earth. The delivery is made and a small crack begins to spread, and all the glass is breaking. All is in shambles. One of the parts left is large enough to rise in order to walk, eat, talk, cry, and sleep, but it is all shattered glass.

I was sleeping in an apartment in San Francisco, thirty miles north of my own home, which is near Stanford University where I have worked the last twenty years. A friend and I had come up to the city for a film festival, a favor that I had promised myself for years. After the first evening, we stayed with my friend Lee, a therapist like me, who was asleep in his bedroom. I was soundly at rest in the spare bedroom, and my friend John who came up with me was on the pull-out couch in the living room. The answering machine was near him, and I did not even hear the phone ring. John woke me, saying that my former wife had left an urgent message to call her. I immediately assumed the worst: that one of my parents had died.

In my reflections over the next two years, I have returned to this assumption often because of what it reveals to me about my soul. Infrequently, my thoughts could entertain through their own momentum the possibility of those close to me dying: parents, siblings, friends, or lovers. However, my psyche had no niche for the death of either of my children. It was not structured to register this information in any a priori category. For twenty-three years since the birth of my daughter, the daily readiness, whether conscious or just below the surface, was one of protection. Once, in rural Rhode Island, when my children where three and two years of age, I was in the front yard working, and the kids were along the side of the house. Suddenly they were gone. There were woods in back of the house. As I ran toward the woods, I saw them hiding in an alcove of the house, my daughter so delighted in having pulled one over on her Dad. The instinctual protective adrenaline—this is what the psyche carries. Not death images of one's children.

Judy, my ex-wife of fourteen years, had been calling into the early morning hours, trying to locate me. Leaving messages with several friends for me to call, she eventually reached Carole, a work colleague and best of friends, who happened to remember a comment I made to her two evenings earlier that I would be up at the film festival and staying with Lee. The location for the delivery had been found.

Of the flashbacks I have had in my grieving, this one is the most frequent. I am told that Andy is dead. I am told that my son was at work, and at 9:00 P.M. the security guard heard a thud and found his body on the parking lot pavement. Andy's office was on the third floor, and it is unknown whether he fell, was pushed, or jumped. I am told he died at Stanford Hospital two hours later, never regaining consciousness.

By the time Judy and her husband Ron were notified and arrived at the hospital, Andy was dead. Judy has the visuals of our son's body, in his broken state, soon after dying. By four o'clock, his body was in the morgue. My flashback is not of visual images, but the voice, those words, as glass begins to crack.

THE RIDE

Being driven down a highway before dawn by John, a friend too young to know the signs of shock, I was silent, oh how deceptively so, as the war in my head began. The brief phone dialogue between Judy and me left me with her horrific impression that Andy had jumped.

After years of teaching, mentoring, and being a therapist for young adults, I now sensed that I might not have even provided the framework from which my own son could find meaning. As my shame engulfed me, I wanted to flee. Sell my home, move away to remoteness in a corner of the world, total radical change, for my life was suddenly revealed as a sham. Memory went to a news account I had read several years earlier of a father, some friends, and a son hunting, separated in the woods. The father saw movement, fired his rifle at what he believed was prey. As the father came upon his slain son, he turned the gun upon himself in a quick and definitive suicide.

Had I done the same, through years of self-deception that I could not or would not let myself view? Jump? He was neither distressed nor facing any crisis, and he was surrounded by family and friends. Sure, he had been overworking in this first year out of college, but so were a lot of other young people in the Silicon Valley. Jump?

My son's death took me back into darkness that I have known too often. Whether through my own dark journeys of the soul, or through having shared the broken and pained lives of patients for twenty-five years, I was weary of the suffering. This ride to a corpse who was my son did not fling me into an unknown hell, only back again into suffering from which I had not found escape. If I was not shocked by the horror, then why was I in total silence, wanting merger into nonexistence?

My own depressions long ago introduced me to despair, but had not prepared me for this type of loss. Andy's death is a line of demarcation. As Western history divides itself by the birth of

Christianity into BC and AD, so also is my own individual life now divided. *AD*, catechism class long ago having provided the mnemonic *after death* and with irony I see my son's initials.

THE CONFUSION

The sun rose early Saturday morning as Judy, Ron, and I sat in the living room of the house Judy and I bought when we had moved to California two decades earlier. What happened? They shared information, starting from the time a call came from the hospital at 11:00 the night before. Andy had been out on the patio near his workspace. Somehow, for some reason, he went into another area from the patio and then jumped or fell off the building's third floor edge to the parking lot below. He hit the pavement at approximately 8:59 P.M., for his watch stopped on impact. Judy and Ron had called him at the office at 8:30 P.M. and left a voicemail message that they were at the shopping center down the street and asked if he wanted to take a break and join them for ice cream. We were later informed that he had listened to the voicemail within that twenty-nine minute interval and had written down their cell phone number, apparently with the intention of calling them back. Speculations with little evidence began to emerge in our discussion. What now?

They had already called our daughter Carrie in Boston and told her of Andy's death without giving details. She was arriving later that morning at the airport. We were all going to pick her up, and I intended to surround her with impermeable protection. There is a scene in a BBC film about death, *Truly, Madly, Deeply*, where Alan Rickford, who is deceased, describes to his beloved wife a playground where a little girl had died. There is a plaque that reads:

> From Alice's Mom and Dad
> In loving memory of Alice
> Who used to play here

Rickford says: "You see the parents take their child off the swing and see the plaque. And they hold on to their sons and daughters so tight, clinging on for dear life. . . ."

My daughter had accepted a teaching job in Colombia, South America, which would start that fall. She had researched well the risks of rebel activity in the part of the country where the school is but was still at odds with her mother who was adamantly opposed to this decision. Carrie is the risk taker. Her brother was not.

There were a few hours before the trip to the airport. I decided to go home and begin the phone calls, the initial few of many to come.

How should one be the bearer of such tidings to family? I worried, given my parents' age, that the shock of this news could be deadly. I phoned my older brother. He was at home. "Andy is dead," I wept. He replied, "I love you, I love you." We have seldom talked with such affection, thus its impact was all the more profound. He said he would travel the few miles to the house where we grew up and my parents still lived. I have never asked him to describe what that scene was like and may never do so.

My friend Carole was also at home on the other side of the Bay. She said she would come immediately. There was no protocol in my mind for the announcement of tragedy, the order of whom to tell, the words to use, the anguish that whispers, *what difference does it make*? My professional colleague and closest friend of twenty-five years, Andy C., answered the phone. After weeping with him in sharing the news, he called back minutes later after he and his wife had absorbed the full impact of our conversation and entered their own grief. Then I made two calls to strangers I had never met: the executive manager of Andy's company, who had left a voicemail, and a call to the detective assigned to the case. Soon after, my mother and father called. They now knew of Andy's death, and my mother was alarmed about my welfare, for I am her son. My father was emotionally overwhelmed. My brother called back. I was not to be alone, he demanded, but there was already knocking at the door. Carole had arrived and would be at my side part of each day for the next week.

The wait at the airport gate for my daughter was the most stressful moment of my life, with the exception of the funeral itself. Before her plane arrived, Judy, Ron, Carole, and I stood in a misshapen circle. I mumbled that I might not be capable of going on without Andy. Judy instinctively responded to me, "You have another child you need to be here for"—an appropriate reprimand, no matter how authentic my despair.

Judy pulled me aside as my friend Carole engaged Ron. She said she intended to direct any of Andy's assets that she would inherit to Carrie. I was confused by this concrete topic in the turbulence of my emotional hurricane. I remembered this moment with some resentment for months to come, the mingling of such intense grief with worries about money. In the twenty years since the divorce, we had not been exempt from the all-too-common pattern for divorced individuals to channel many of their unresolved issues into fights about money. But in a moment when we had lost so much, there was a resistant voice that said, *Don't. Not now.* But I was too disoriented to express it.

Passengers arrived as relatives waited, a commonplace scenario for urbanites. Carole sensed my body tense as my daughter walked out of the gate and whispered to me, "This will be the hardest moment of your life, be brave." Half of my children were not present and never would be again. Judy and I embraced Carrie simultaneously, and we wept unabashedly as strangers looked on in momentary curiosity.

While finally walking to the baggage area, my daughter asked more about the manner of Andy's death. Her mother answered so starkly, "He jumped." I was struck by a wave of devastation that passed over Carrie's distorted features as she sobbed further. She was now an only child and had just been told that Andy had chosen that.

THE PLANNING

A couple of years before my son's death, I had been listening to a report on National Public Radio about families having to make decisions about coffins, burials, flowers, etc., in a short period of time and amidst initial waves of grief. The broadcast went on to discuss the funeral industry's advantageous financial position during such periods. The program mentioned a non-profit consumer group that addressed such concerns and provided advice on the importance of anticipating such decisions and the need to plan for contingencies in advance. After having listened to the report, I found their Web page[1] and asked my older brother

---

[1] http://www.funerals.org

to also take a look so that we might avoid any future involving significant monetary decisions while under duress. Of course, at the time I had been thinking about the eventual deaths of my parents.

Here I was back in Judy's living room Saturday afternoon less than eighteen hours after Andy's fall, needing to face such a totally unfamiliar set of tasks. Not once during this afternoon of planning did I recall my preemptory efforts at avoiding funeral complications from two years earlier. Questions of *when* and *where* to have the funeral were first to arise, but no clear criteria emerged to guide us, and no one in the room had enough experience in burials to offer explicit suggestions. Our parents and their ability to travel were highly relevant for the *when*. Being part of a community, as I am at Stanford, proved to be an enormous asset in the days to follow concerning the *where* and *how*. Issues involving catering, lack of parking, bussing people, the printing of programs and various other tasks were all facilitated greatly by my friends at the University.

However, as we plodded through the afternoon, one person in particular provided clarity around choices. For the prior two years, I had worked with the Offices of Religious Life and Residential Life at Stanford to develop workshops for students who had experienced a significant death in their families. We had been concerned that young people in grief who were returning to campus did not have enough peers who had experienced significant loss to fully understand bereavement and be patient enough to provide them support. Reverend Kelly Denton-Berhaug, an Episcopal priest on the Religious Life staff, was on the working committee with me. I decided to contact her and was immediately struck by her seasoned composure in the face of tragedy. Though with her own family during a weekend, she immediately insisted on driving down the forty miles to be with us as we stumbled along with our numerous questions in planning an event that only lurks in most parents' nightmares.

By the afternoon's end, we had a place: Memorial Church, on the campus where Andy had graduated the year before. We finally had a day: Friday, a week after his death. We chose a group of four additional celebrants to join Kelly in officiating the service. Perhaps the most profound gesture during this entire ordeal was how Kelly responded to us during a few critical choice points. Since we intended to have Andy's body resting in a coffin at the service, the event was a funeral and not a memorial service. There are some restrictions against funerals at this church in the will of one of the University's founders, Mrs. Jane Stanford. Kelly paused, reflected a moment, and then stated unequivocally, "We will find a way." In an afternoon of deep emotional and existential challenges, this priestess intuitively knew that no red tape should compromise the essential needs on the table. A century before, the Stanfords themselves had created the University in memory of their only son who had died in his late teens. Memorial Church was created as a sacred space to mourn and honor a beloved son. Now it was our turn to be there.

In deciding who would be the celebrants, I knew how awkward and transparent it could be when a minister or priest delivered a eulogy about a deceased individual who was not well known to them. I did not want Andy's remembrance to be so compromised. Both Judy and I were friends with Sid, a man who was a Catholic priest but left his active role in the church twenty years prior to marry a former Catholic nun, Audrey. They both knew Andy from his years as a youth when he and I had joined Sid and his brother in watching Notre Dame football on Saturdays. Audrey also works in the same school district as Judy. Though now a laicized priest, Sid, through his own spiritual energy and devotion, officiates in many church functions. He was our choice to provide the sermon. Besides Kelly, the other three celebrants were all friends of ours who knew Andy was our son, but had not known him personally.

Andy was surrounded by educators in his family. Judy, her husband Ron, and I are all accustomed to public speaking. In the intensely disorienting grief during the next few days, I was surprised at how we instinctively decided that our voices needed to be heard as we tried to envision how to memorialize Andy. We also sensed that Andy's Stanford friends would want a forum to express their clear devotion to their friend. His sister deferred a speaker's role in favor of being a reader, her grief complicated with the intensities and competition that these siblings stirred within each other. And so, throughout the week, we sketched out the logistics for players in the tragic drama called a funeral.

THE FIRST NIGHT

The first night after Andy's death, there was a sharing which resulted in unexpected comfort and attachment. Carole had been with me since the morning. Dan, my friend with whom Carole had been in contact, came up to the house and spent the night with me so Carole could exit later in the evening. Most important to me was that Lexy, Allan, and Jason were there, to be with the father of their best friend. All three had known Andy since junior high, spent high school together, and, while Jason went to college in Texas, the other three went on to Stanford. Their loss was of a beloved friend whom they had known half their lives, through three levels of education, and for two of them, their current roommate.

Comfort came in the stories they told. Carole was the unofficial moderator, a role she was born to play. Though never having met these three young people before, she bonded with them quickly and elicited details in a relaxed rhythm about my son that most fathers might never have heard. His silliness around dinner preparations and the rationale of why he typically only chose black, gray, white, and dark blue clothing. Stories of his generosity. Tears made their way out, but what brought some peace in the midst of my pain was laughter and joy in the remembrances. Where were the descriptions of his distress, angst, desperation? None emerge. Had deep troubles been so thoroughly disguised?

I had heard in the early hours of that Saturday that my son is not alive. Lexy and Allan waited for their roommate who never came home. Lexy is the more expressive of the three, Jason ready to supply wit, and Allan the quietest and perhaps most similar to Andy in his deeper introversion. We would not have gathered but for this tragedy, yet there we sat. Two generations linked by my role as a parent, a role now permanently altered by Andy's absence.

The first night after Andy's sudden death unfolded in a senseless order. Being alone would have been tough. Being with others required some responsibility, but such energy breaks up the numbness—a resistance to floating away into oblivion.

Everyone eventually left, with the exception of Dan. He slept next to me, as an anchor.

THE COMPANY

The Director was the onsite managing executive of my son's employer and had left a voicemail for me to call her. Later on, I realized what a terrible call it must have been for her to make. However, when I first called her, I was furious. My conversation from just two evenings before with my own colleagues had been focused on how hard these companies push young eager graduates, and I channeled all my resentments toward her company as I heard the first explanation from them of what had happened. I listened in stony silence as she told me that Andy had been working late Friday night. His last co-worker had left at about 8:30 P.M. The security guard heard a thump during his rounds outside the building. He found Andy's body. She tells me Andy had gone to a *maintenance area* on the roof, and this was where the *fall* happened. I visualized her descriptions. I imagined air conditioning equipment and other machinery on this roof area and did not understand why Andy would have been out there unless he had intended to jump.

I asked about signs that might have indicated distress at work, particularly any unusual events that day, trying to get any information that could shed light on an apparent desperation of which no one was aware. "None," she replied

She added that he had seemed himself and that there were no indications of mood change or odd behavior. We said little else at this time. She was being genuinely empathetic, but her energy did not touch me. We agreed that there should be a meeting. Either she or Judy had already given me the name of the detective whom I should call.

A year before, Andy had been weighing an important professional decision. He had been offered a position in an investment bank in Los Angeles in addition to this position with the firm. There was quite a contrast between these two opportunities. The bank job paid more, but probably would have been more hours per week and more stressful, and there would have been a narrower focus for further career choices. He had intended to return for his MBA as a next step, which would allow him to finally move away from his hometown area. By having gone to Stanford, he had denied himself that opportunity. The firm, founded by Stanford economists, offered consulting services to law firms involved in complicated financial and business-related cases that benefit from economic analysis of case material. Andy had seen the advantages of this position as representing a higher learning curve of material that he had not yet been exposed to in school, a more informal environment, and the chance to transfer to their New York office after a couple of years. He bit the bullet to remain in the Bay Area and was excited about joining this firm. He had made a good decision to choose September rather than July as the start date for his first professional job and took the summer to relax.

The firm's building is in the heart of Menlo Park, less than a mile from where Andy had gone to high school, just a few miles from Stanford, and closer still to my previous home where I had raised the children in joint custody with their mom. The facility has a stone marker in the shape of a bell on the lawn that displays their name. Andy was very pleased to have been working there, and I also enjoyed a sense of pride when I passed the building, knowing how competitive the process was for such a position and how hard Andy had worked. The building remains the same, but for me it has come to symbolize a very different emotion than that of admiration.

I had visited Andy's office on a Sunday after his first several months there. The firm leased the second and third floors, with Andy's office being on the latter. One needed a security code to enter the elevator from the garage level and to access these two floors. He gave me the tour, including his office itself, which was on one of the outer walls and had a window that looked out onto an outside deck area. This was possible, because the first two stories are a larger rectangle than the third floor, which is smaller in size. Therefore, the roof of the second floor extended beyond the third floor perimeter, resulting in an outside deck area on each side of the third floor beyond the windows. Tables and chairs allowed a pleasant area for lunch or a place to catch a breath of fresh air.

As a very polished firm used to working with high-powered law firms, they responded to the tragedy of my son's death in very gracious ways. Flowers were delivered to my home, as well as delicatessen food for out-of-town guests. Several months after Andy's death, there was a dinner for Judy and me with all of Andy's co-workers, in which we were presented with a book they had made in his memory. The book included photos, anecdotes that they elaborated upon at the dinner, and samples of his work.

The dilemma for me during all these empathetic gestures from real people was my ambivalence about the motives of the decision-makers given the data, impressions, and multiple questions that were to emerge during our visit to the firm two days after Andy's death. However, a year later, when a grant fund for volunteer projects was set up at Stanford in Andy's name and it fell short of meeting the $50,000 minimum needed to be a continual endowment, the Director made a generous personal donation to close the gap.

THE DETECTIVE

A good friend who teaches drama at Holy Cross and is a movie critic for one of Boston's newspapers had once been visiting in the Bay Area for an evening. During his visit, we watched one of his favorite television shows that I had not seen before, *Law and Order*. Since I enjoyed the show, he later sent me twelve episodes that he had taped, and I watched them over a period of a few months. Each episode began at the scene of a crime, many of them gruesome, and though I had originally viewed the show as only entertainment, on some very subtle level I began feeling uneasy. I stopped viewing the show by late spring—probably a month before Andy's death. These repeated stories of police investigations, even though biased through the Hollywood lens, shaped the questions I asked when the detective assigned to Andy's case took us to the scene of his death.

The detective was not in when I called Saturday morning, several hours after first having learned about my son's death. He called back mid-morning. He had not yet visited the scene of the incident and had only briefly reviewed the report from the officer who had responded to the security guard's 911 call. He was not much more informed than I. He repeated the Director's understanding that Andy had left his office and went out onto a maintenance area and fell to his death from the roof. He made some implicit remark about Andy's judgment. He did ask me some initial questions about my son's recent emotional disposition, to which I could not provide any unusual answers. The most I could say was that I knew he was putting in a lot of hours and seemed tired. The detective insinuated that certain individuals just seem to snap, to which I did not comment. What I did say to him was that I wanted to be kept informed of all the evidence that came in, no matter in what direction it pointed.

The next day I first met the police detective as he walked into the room at the firm. Ron whispered, "Oh boy, we have a cowboy."

THE VISIT

As Ron, Judy, and I met later Saturday and into Sunday, we became less and less impressed with how the official system was handling the event of our son's death. In contacting the County Coroner's Office, we discovered from a secretary that the case had mistakenly been marked as a suicide even though the initial police report had listed it as "undetermined" and still under investigation. The death certificate might have been marked as a suicide had we not talked with the coroner on Monday, who immediately recognized the mistake and reclassified it as *undetermined*, awaiting both the police investigation as well as his own. There can be serious consequences for families who do not track the system to catch bureaucratic blunders. We knew that a face-to-face meeting was necessary with the detective and the Director to address all our emerging questions, so we set one up to be held at the firm's office building. Besides Judy, Ron, and me, our daughter Carrie, Lexy, Allan, and Jason completed our group of seven.

Judy, Ron, and I developed a list of questions we wanted to pursue with the Director. Given how intense the three of us felt just talking among ourselves, we did not want to appear too confrontational. Our plan was first to hear the detective's summary and any further information the Director was willing to disclose from the company's knowledge of the events. We also were concerned that issues of liability were likely to be on the minds of any person who represented the employer. Our questions were:

Was Andy's office locked from the outside?
Were there any saved messages on his voicemail?
Is there any way to ascertain messages that he had listened to and deleted?

What voicemail messages were not picked up by Andy?

Is there a way to find out phone conversations?

What e-mails were posted that day? Is the server secure? Might there be something deleted that was upsetting to him?

Are you aware of any upsetting interchanges with Andy during the last week?

Who was his new supervisor? When was she or he assigned? And what was his relationship like with this new supervisor?

What was he working on at the time?

What interactions were there with colleagues, clients that day?

Can you tell us about his last performance review?

Was there a life insurance policy?

Judy and I met the Director outside the locked building a few minutes before 2:00 on Sunday afternoon. She was very professional in appearance and greeted us with more openness than I had anticipated. I was angry inside but contained it. The others eventually arrived, except the detective, and we all went into the building and up to the company's conference room. There was no formal conversation until the detective arrived and began his spiel. His major theme, emphasized in several ways, was that the investigation was just beginning, he did not have a lot of information with which to respond to our questions, and that it might be four to six weeks until the investigation was completed. The Director had no new information and responded to our range of questions with no data that revealed any unusual occurrences in Andy's work environment prior to his death, and she only had positive feedback about the quality of his work. The only observation that at all related to a concern was that Andy himself might have underestimated his own high quality of output, despite evaluations to the contrary. With this portion of the meeting completed, we rose to go to the third floor to see his office and the site of his fall.

As several of us were walking with the detective, he attempted to show empathy by saying that his thirteen year-old daughter recently had a school friend who had committed suicide and how hard that had been on the family, but then lectured us about it being too early to speculate. The detective was not a good card player—he had tipped his hand during this onsite visit and revealed his biases. Ron's suggested cowboy image was a much more accurate description of the detective than that of a professional with investigative competence.

Another surprising and revealing observation about the attitude the police were apparently taking was that Andy's office was not secured. There was no yellow police tape. The firm itself had simply put up a hand-made sign indicating "No entrance." Any evidence surrounding his workspace, the last location he had been in, could intentionally or unintentionally have been altered. What awaited us next, though, entirely changed the path we had been heading down the last thirty-six hours.

We were escorted out onto the deck on the roof area outside Andy's office via a sliding glass door in the manager's office. Like mummies being unwrapped and startled by light, the seven of us were jolted out of our distorted images of how this site might look. We stood on an attractive wooden deck with a patio table and chairs that were bordered on three sides by an area again as large as the deck that was covered by egg-shaped rocks, about the size of squashes. This rock area was then bordered by the edge of the building. There was a railing around the deck, about waist high with a parallel rail knee high, with a gate that had a small thumb latch.

Of most interest to me were the flat patio stones that formed a path from the gate onto the oval rocks and led to the roof's perimeter. I turned to the Director with a growing sense of incredulity and asked, "Why is this called a maintenance area when there is a stone path inviting walkers?" Her reply was, "The patio walk stones are intended for people who wash the windows." I then inquired (only half expecting a reply) if the firm had issued any written policy or oral prohibitions to employees about not going onto the stoned area or avoiding it as a maintenance area. To her credit, she was direct and non-evasive: "No."

There was no maintenance machinery on the rooftop. There were no "Do not enter" signs on chain-link fences. There was only an appealing deck area with a surrounding rock garden and walkway for employees to enjoy. The detective led Judy and me toward the spot where Andy had fallen, saying as we approached, "Be careful, the footing is very dangerous." Since I had dress loafers on and had not been walking along the flat patio stones, but rather directly upon the rocks, I indeed had slipped a couple of times. The detective went on to say to the two of us, "Even I become disoriented here."

The roof's edge did not have a typical half-wall barrier. (We were to later learn that the current building code required a minimum wall of forty-two inches.) Instead it had a lip of only eighteen inches, which came up to mid-shin level. Lexy later commented that the low height of this lip might be more likely to cause someone to trip than prevent him or her from falling. When the three of us returned to the deck, Lexy did ask the detective if any footprints were found on the ledge's lip, and he replied that none had been found.

As the others went back inside, questions rushed through my mind. The detective had given no signs that he welcomed an inquisitive, wounded father. Detectives are not on the informal list of *Helping Professionals* we carry in our heads, and understandably so. Their turf is a tough one and wearing emotions on the sleeve does not work. However, I did expect him to be responsive to logic. I asked about the differences between where a body would land if it fell versus if it jumped or was pushed. The detective understood such a line of questioning as an unintended challenge and made some comment about police work not being like it is shown on television. Maybe I had watched too many episodes of *Law and Order*, but the same questions were later posed by legal experts. As we left the deck, he countered my lines of inquiry: "This is not a homicide. I am doing you a courtesy by bringing you up and showing you the site." So much for his prelude a half an hour before that this was the beginning of the investigation.

In the midst of shock and pure grief, I experienced an adrenaline rush. Why? My initial horror that my son may have taken his own life was now very much in doubt as I examined the site of his death. Years later, I still ponder this reaction. My present interpretation is that though the hole ripped into my heart will never be filled again, there was a dispersal of both the shame about suicide and the confusion about how I could have failed him so much as a father. This is an understandable emotional reaction for a father, not typical for a clinician. As a therapist, I do not consciously judge a parent whose child has died through suicide differently than a parent who lost a child through an accident. However, the intrinsic emotional relief I felt and communicated to those close to me in the several days after the visit to the deck area indicates that I do on some personal level operate with such judgment.

When I was a young professional in the mid-1970s, I attended an eight-day conference on healing. This workshop had a significant impact on my development. One of the participants was a minister who had lost his twenty-five-year-old son to suicide. This had clearly taken a heavy toll on the father. An image he shared was: *If hospitals have emergency rooms where they accept all who are in danger, would not heaven have such a room for those who took their own life?* I was very moved by this image, particularly in its challenge to conceive a depth of mercy beyond the constraints of institutional dogma. *Agape*, God's unconditional love, is the manna that feeds the despairing. Shame and guilt may be uninvited guests to the emotional gathering when facing the reality of a deceased child, and if so present, they cannot be dismissed. Traumatic deaths of our children by suicide or through the violence of others add additional folds to the *burial robes*. The courage of parents in facing such realities is heroic. The growing realization that my son had not despaired was of significance to me in facing my loss, but a death by suicide provides no evaluation of parenting. How we bring up our children is too complex a process to be reduced to such simple judgments.

A visit two days later by a colleague from work resulted in a discussion about a dream that was powerful corroborating evidence of my thoughts leading away from suicide as the cause of death.

THE DREAM

A good friend, who is a psychiatrist, visited on Tuesday to help prepare the house for my family's arrival from out of town. Humility speaks clearly when such a talented university peer comes over ready to clean the floors, etc. As we chatted out on my deck, she told me that her mom had had a dream about Andy two evenings before. Her mother had only caught a brief fragment of the dream, but Andy was talking to her and saying that *I am all right, and it's not what they think. . . .*

My friend's mother had never met Andy and only had met me quite briefly on two occasions. This fact is important as there was no personal history with him upon which the dream could be based. Therefore, I interpreted the dream to be synchronistic. Jungian psychology uses the term synchronicity to describe when an external event corresponds to images in an individual's internal life in a powerful manner that cannot be explained by cause and effect. Andy's death did not cause her dream to occur, nor did this woman, not associated to our lives in any significant manner, have the emotional context to typically trigger such a dream. Yet, the two are related, by more than simple chance.

I intuitively understood the dream. *Andy's okay and we needn't be distracted by others' first impressions.*

No other response had done what this dream had done for my grief.

THE INFORMING

Back home the evening after Andy death, I began to call those whom I judged needed to know and listened to the numerous messages left on my answering machine. What were my expectations of good friends as I voiced such terrible news? Was there anything, after momentary silence, which could have made a difference to my increasing numbness? Could any of their emotions have bridged the gap that had cast me as such a tragic figure? There were perceivable differences among them as I placed these calls.

Four of my friends—two different couples—had lost children years before. Gene and Nancy's young son, Gavin, died of leukemia before age five, only shortly after I had moved to California with my young children. Mary and Ed had lost all three of their boys to muscular dystrophy over a period of twenty-five years. That their marriages have survived puts them into a statistical minority of couples who lose a child. Their responses were different from others I received. They were already initiated long ago into the unique club of parents who survive their children. They were not thrown off balance by such news but had deep pores to absorb all the implications of such a tragedy. They kindly only mentioned a few ramifications to start. They knew that I had crossed over a line of no return and that any innocence that may have survived into adulthood was now gone forever.

In the week preceding the funeral, I spent several late evenings planning funeral events at Judy's house and dealing with the bureaucracy of the coroners, bank, insurance, and the police. As many as twenty-five messages awaited me on my answering machine each night as word of Andy's death spread. Some people were surprised that I listened to each of these phone messages during those initial evenings of emotional intensity. It actually never occurred to me not to hear how others were reaching out to me, no matter how hesitant and limited their messages might be.

Years before, when I was slightly older than my own son, my advisor at my alma mater lost one of his daughters in a terrible car accident involving several Notre Dame coeds. He had concluded from his experience of grief that it was important that others say something—it didn't matter what. For him, someone's silence was more isolating and confusing than any verbal attempt to express sympathy. He knew some friends hesitated because they felt unable to find words *profound* enough to match the depth of the tragedy of losing a child. His need was not for condensed wisdom, but contact. *Say something—anything is better than no response,* he would lament. This advice has always stuck with me, and I have since then approached aggrieved friends with some comment, no matter how awkward I felt. So now, as I stood in an empty kitchen, the grieving father, I wanted to honor those friends and acquaintances by listening to them.

The response to sharing the news of Andy's death that had the greatest impact upon me was from my former TA at Stanford and friend, Casey. Initially, I was not able to call him because he had left for a trip to Europe several days prior to Andy's death. He called me unexpectedly from Germany on the following Tuesday, inquiring about the itinerary of a mutual friend whom he had planned to meet in Paris. He knew from the first syllable out of my mouth that something was wrong. Beginning to cry, I revealed the tragedy. Casey had known Andy from a few projects on my house that the three of us had worked on together. Casey immediately said he would fly back to be with me. I advised him against it since he had just arrived in Europe and assured him that I would have plenty of support over the next several days. Two days later he called back, his tickets for a flight back in hand. He arrived after the funeral but just in time to join the circle of friends that followed. Casey had limited funds, but he came. His decision to return meant he was able to hold me, share meals between the crying, and provide some youthful energy to that suddenly vacated with Andy's absence. He stayed a week before flying back, and I will neither forget his selflessness through this gesture nor the challenge for me to sacrifice in the same degree for others who are grieving.

The question of when friends who live some distance away should come after a death is relevant. The ritual power of wakes and funerals inheres in their being timely in bringing together mourners. However, for those who did not directly know the deceased but are reaching out to someone left behind, their presence at the rituals may be of less value than a later visit when the primary mourners are left alone as others return to their work-a-day worlds. In my case, two friends living in different places on the East Coast decided to delay their trips out to be with me until a month to six weeks later. This postponement saved me from extended isolation in the weeks that followed the funeral.

There is a large body of information concerning historical and cross-cultural traditions surrounding childhood death. In his recent memoir about the loss of his college age daughter, *Courtney's Legacy: A Father's Journey* (2001), George Cantor has provided an insightful chapter chronicling differences in customs of mourning. In our case a particular example was when my daughter went to Ecuador about two months after Andy's death. She had planned this visit as the beginning of her year teaching in Colombia. Certainly the circumstances and emotions surrounding the visit had changed, and though she withdrew from the job, she decided to make the two-week trip to Ecuador. Carrie would be staying with the host family she had lived with during her junior year study abroad. She retained close ties to the family, and both parties were looking forward to their first reunion in three years.

While there, Carrie observed a difference in the nature of their reactions to Andy's death compared to those of her family and friends in the United States. Though no less sympathetic, the context of their comments originated from a culture where the line between life and death was much more fluid. Her family had responded with concern, but expressed none of the shock and outrage that such an event could or should happen to a twenty-two year old. Carrie recalled how when she was attending college there, a professor had once asked for a show of hands of those who had lost immediate family in transportation-related accidents. She was stunned when a majority of students raised their hands.

She had also celebrated *Dia de los Muertes*, the Day of the Dead. This holiday, common in many Latin American countries, features special blood-colored fruit drinks, brightly decorated skulls, and people-shaped breads. The mood of the ritual is one of remembrance but also festivity and humor, casting grieving for the dead in a different hue. In a country where even those not facing crushing poverty are harried by economic and political instability, death is not only more common, but more integrated into the natural cycle of life. That death remains confined to the realm of the elderly was a luxurious belief that few could afford. For Judy and me, the realization that by limiting our family to two children we were vulnerable to instantly having half of them die, or even having no children left at all, was not in our consciousness. As an American who was living with economic and political stability, I was lured into a naïve assumption that my children would outlive me. Probability was on my side. The intrinsically ephemeral nature of life itself was not.

Some predictable consequences of informing others were their sympathetic responses: food, flowers, cards and more cards, and the donations to our designated charity. I was deeply touched to find in my mailbox on Saturday afternoon, just a half day after my son's death, a hand-delivered card. It was from my friends John and Abel, both of whom are in my running group. John had originally driven me back from San Francisco during the pre-dawn hours following Andy's death, and the roundtrip drive to my house this afternoon was not a short one for him.

I did, however, notice a difference in the amount of flowers and food between Judy's and my house as the days proceeded. Since both she and Ron were very involved in their community through their professional activities as school administrators, the high volume of goods was apparent to me, particularly because we had been using their home as the planning site during the week. My community was the university, and specifically the health center where I work, which had organized a very systematic group response. I also lived miles into the redwoods, essentially without neighbors, so there were no spontaneous knocks on the door from neighbors with casserole dishes.

Having never been in the role of a key grieving family member, I did not have any experiential map to bring with me through this maze. When we are in shock, our regression elicits wounded parts in our psyche that can be dormant for years, then rise on such occasions. This childlike experience of *who is getting more holiday presents* I found curious and a bit embarrassing when in the midst of such a deep grief. Why did I notice and react to such insignificant comparisons? The flames of loss that were scorching me had not burned away all my foibles. There was part of me that was still a *hurt child* inside even as the tragedy demanded my fullest adult capacities.

THE WAKE

My family arrived from Detroit on Wednesday, the day before the wake—two brothers, two sisters-in-law, and my parents. For the first time, I was not at the airport picking up family. My workplace arranged an SUV for them to rent, and they made their way down the peninsula and into the woods on their own. Greeting them at the front door was an anxious moment for me—this first face-to-face contact with family since Andy's death. Blood ties us through time and has transcended many lifestyle differences, and yet I knew we would be handling grief in very different ways throughout the next several days. Since the death of a child was such uncharted territory for all of us, the cues and scripts were unknown. I suggested that despite the deep pain and sadness, we needed to be able to talk about day-to-day issues and ease our tensions with humor and distractions. My older brother later remarked to me that this had been very helpful in reducing the self-consciousness that such gatherings elicited in us new initiates to grief.

The location of the funeral home happened to be across the street from my therapist's office. For the previous year I had parked in front of this building, without having given it any particular notice until maybe several months before Andy's death. As with my watching the television show *Law and Order*, I had a slight intuitive reaction that I had barely noted, but which had prompted me to look more often at the building, though at the time I had dismissed these subtle reactions. This building was the place where we saw my son's body for the last time.

A critical decision that Judy and I had to make several days before the wake was whether there should be an open or closed casket. She wanted the former. I wanted a closed one. We were told that the damage to the back of Andy's head from his fall could be made presentable. I deferred to her choice but suggested that at the funeral the casket be closed. My concern about an open casket was that there might be too great a divergence between how others and I remembered Andy and the prepared body that lay in the casket. I sensed that Judy needed to literally see Andy more, that she was not yet ready to release the visual contact with him. The immediate family viewed the body about a half an hour before the public arrived. As Judy, Carrie, Ron, and I entered the largest of their chapels, Judy's choice was validated. Andy's appearance was very similar to my impressions of him alive.

In studying liturgy and rituals as an undergraduate, I had learned that energy within them is best elicited when a balance between structure and spontaneity is achieved. I have been to weddings that are aesthetically beautiful but the vitality was structured out of them. On the other hand, social gatherings that lack thoughtfulness for the nourishing and comforting of the guests are usually not saved by pure spontaneity. For the wake, I wanted to err in the direction of openness, allowing those who knew Andy a chance to be expressive. Since Carrie decided against giving a talk at his funeral the next day, we had suggested that she address the guests after Kelly opened the ritual with prayer. We had a small reception line that passed before the body. Visitors then sat in one of the forty or so rows of pews. There was an open microphone from which Carrie invited anyone who wanted to share remarks to come forward. I asked ahead of time if this was their largest room, which it was, for I was concerned that it might become overcrowded. I was assured that since wakes are open periods, as ours was from 8:00 P.M. to 10:00 P.M., there would be a constant flow of people in and out. They had not previously experienced problems with capacity.

Wrong. As Andy's and our friends arrived and arrived and arrived, those who preceded them did not leave, largely due to the powerful ongoing narratives being shared at the open microphone. Story after story, small anecdotes, touching verses of praise, and tearful expressions of gratitude honored this young man. Fortunately, the lobby outside the chapel had speakers in it that relayed these testimonies, for some guests were not able to get into the chapel at all. Carrie, Lexy, and some of Andy's other friends had spent part of the week gathering numerous photos of him that spanned his twenty-two short years. They reprinted them on three large white poster boards that were on easels in the lobby, so the later guests at least were able to hear the verbal tapestry and see an abridged photo history of this boy-man.

Unlike the funeral the next day, that night we parents had silent roles. Standing with some required formality, but in such grief, I simultaneously greeted the endless flow of mourners while listening to the continual eulogies from those speaking at the podium. I had not thought ahead of time about whom I might see at the wake and was surprised at the diversity. Besides expected friends and acquaintances, I welcomed a patient from my private practice, the contractor who had worked on my house, my dentist who was also Andy's, and parents of childhood friends of Andy that I had not seen in years. There were many people I did not know who were there for Judy and Ron. So here, at this most intimate time of tragedy, there were gathered so many who were part of my life, mixed among strangers, mostly silent, as the narration echoed in the stillness of the parlor.

Family members were seated in the front pew. I knew that Judy's parents, being more introverted, would not be sharing any of their thoughts publicly. I anticipated that my older brother, who also teaches at the college level, would speak and he did. After telling about Andy's caring role as an older cousin to his own son, he finished by reading a letter that one of his fifteen year-old twin daughters had sent to Carrie and me. She wrote:

Dear Uncle Doug and Carrie,
I am not sure how to start this letter. I am very sorry and very
sad about what happened to Andy. He was great. Matt really
looked up to him like an older brother, which was awesome for
him because otherwise he only has two sisters. I will miss him a
lot too. I always had fun with him whenever he would visit
and when we came to visit you. I am trying to look at this
remembering that God takes people when they are spiritually
ready and have given everything they have to the people around
them. Andy must have been a great, great person in order to

have been taken from us so soon. I am sure that we will see him
again some day, when God thinks we are ready.
Love,
Julia

My father, as it turned out, was the last to speak. He is a storyteller, though he might not refer to himself by that title. He sold cars most of his life, and when I was a child in suburban Detroit, he was several times the top yearly Ford salesman in the country. His success came from treating his customers well and looking out for their interests. He adored Andy, his first grandson, who was interested in stocks, finance, and the economy, more so than any of his three sons. Also, Andy closely followed professional sports— the entertainment which has always been of daily interest to my father. I am sure he had neither anticipated speaking nor had predetermined what he might say, but his natural oral skills surfaced, and he told a story about a time when Andy was young and he had taken him to purchase baseball cards. He had talked a bit too long by the time he was into his second story about the movies he had taped and tried to convince us to watch when the kids and I visited. The *Flower Drum Song* was his favorite for us because it was a classic movie about San Francisco. Therefore, by his logical deduction, family members from the Bay Area would be naturally inclined to want to see it, no matter how many times he had shown it to us before. He, in particular, had tried to persuade Andy to watch it because Andy stayed up into the wee hours in the recreation room watching sports or other programming. He had even tried bribing Andy with hard cash. As he came to this point in his story, he started to tear up, and in a sudden change of affect, simply said, "And I will never show that film again." Then he sat down. My father had spontaneously shifted roles from storyteller to grandfather, having revealed his broken heart without intent or missing a beat.

The most unexpected aspect of the wake for me was not directly related to the viewing and honoring of Andy but was an unconscious phrase that passed from my lips to my ex-wife. It happened right before the opening of the doors of the chapel after we, the immediate family, had our private viewing. Judy and I were preparing for the reception, and I had approached her and whispered with tears, "Our lives have not been easy, I love you."

The content of this phrase is not unusual, but the context was. Judy and I had been divorced for fifteen years, and she had remarried. Our challenges while together had been formidable, from my disclosure before we were engaged that I was also sexually attracted to men (though at that time without experience), to our struggles during the marriage to find and maintain our common fields of passion.

Since the divorce, we had raised our children jointly and well, but had not remained friends. I have harbored several unhealed wounds inflicted by her, and I have no doubt she has pain remaining from my actions. Parenting is our remaining bond, but not emotional intimacy. Clearly, in the caverns of my psyche, there flourishes caring and sentiment that I had not allowed to be in my awareness for a decade and a half. The depth of this pain, as I readied myself in a reception line that was not celebrating joy but terrible loss, jarred loose deeper emotional attachment. This pairing of *loss with attachment* was a theme that I returned to throughout my long period of grieving.

As the many friends filed out of the chapel, the family remained at the casket. Sid, the former priest who would be speaking at the funeral, stood observing in the background and rightly sensed that we were rookies, not knowing how to act in these moments before the casket was permanently closed. He emerged on his own initiative to lead a prayer—not allowing a purely secular closing to be our final gesture at this wake.

THE FUNERAL

Eleven o'clock in the morning on Friday, June 25th, 1999. I am a strong man physically. Emotionally, I have often lived in the realm of the wounded-healer and have faced suffering within my patients and myself. However, what was required of me to take my daughter's hand and walk down the aisle of Memorial Church that morning followed by the casket of my deceased son, was asking more of me than I thought I could bear. I began to be short of breath and needed to still the inner storm long enough to be able to walk. Of all the uncountable moments of this tragedy that had piled up upon one another, the first several steps of the funeral procession was the closest I had come to breaking. With the contorted face of pure grief and breathing deeply, I marched the march of the dead, the first movement of a larger dance called mourning.

The immediate family was seated in the first pew on the right. I made sure my friends Carole and Andy C. were seated right behind me. Memorial Church is the non-sectarian place of worship that the Stanfords built in the center of their proud university. A large beautiful building, damaged both in the 1906 and 1989 earthquakes, it reopened in 1992 after three years of renovations. Masses of people were seated inside, with more arriving by the minute, until the entire main body of the church was full with over three hundred people. An organist played music from a very large pipe organ in the balcony. We had arranged for the services of the main organist but later discovered at the last minute he could not be there, and a younger woman substituted for him. A week later she wrote me a note indicating that she had been our organist. I remembered her well—I had helped her deal with the untimely death of her older brother when she had been a student.

The casket was wheeled in by the pallbearers, all young friends of Andy, and they positioned themselves in front of the altar. The five clergy we had chosen preceded us into the church and were now presiding at the altar. After the opening prayers, Sid delivered his homily. Despite having been on the sophisticated ground of Stanford, his remarks were not intellectually refined, but heartfelt reflections revealing Sid's strong faith of Andy's continued existence in the realm of a loving God. In remembering him, Sid made reference to Andy's summer with the Los Amigos de las Americas Program, which supported health projects in Latin America: "I like valedictorians who also dig ditches for latrines."

Carrie was the first to read, two poems by Marianne Williamson and Rossiter Worthington Raymond, both of which were untitled. The second reading, which I had chosen, was memorized and delivered by Andy's friend Oliver and was the last paragraph from the chapter "Late Thoughts" in C. G. Jung's *Memories, Dreams, Reflections.* My son's former girlfriend, Ayanna, read a passage from Isaiah for the third reading. I was to be next, the first of five eulogies. I kept reminding myself to heed my advice to Carrie earlier: to allow there to be ample time between readings and not to let anxiety rush you.

TRIBUTE TO MY SON
ANDREW DAHER
JUNE 25, 1999

The last time I was in this Church, this sacred space, to honor a young man's life was the Memorial Vigil for Matthew Shepherd the previous fall. A poignant commentary on how our society had fallen short, resulting in such a horrible death, might have read:

> History shows that members of a community often strive toward uniformity. Indeed, our darkest chronicles and our contemporary headlines relate how groups of people have plotted the extinction of others perceived as somehow different from themselves. Why the desire for "abnormality" to be eliminated? Is it because the unknown or unfamiliar breeds fear? Through the expression of this drive toward conformity, society inevitably develops hatred. In order to avoid such contempt, individuals often choose the course deemed acceptable by a community. Yet, all human beings were not meant to follow a singular route in their lives. As C.S. Lewis once reflected, "humanity does not always pass through phases as a train passes through stations; being alive it has the privilege of always moving yet never leaving anything behind."

That was what my son Andy wrote as a sixteen year-old student as the first paragraph on his college admissions application. A mere boy of sixteen, reflecting upon his community's fear of difference.

In teaching my students here throughout the years, I often say to them that it is the challenge of each new generation to go beyond the boundaries of the consciousness of their parents. I have said to my closest friends, on more than one occasion, that Andy has developed into a better man than I. With razor sharp perceptiveness, he carried his emotions in a manner that seldom let his own wants take precedence over the needs of those around him, friends or strangers. He somehow, I quite frankly don't know how, combined the passionate intensity and energy of his paternal grandfather (an intensity he named "bubbly blood") and the patience and reserved dignity of his maternal grandfather, with an alchemist's wisdom. A synergy emerged of deep intensity that was private, yet always non-threatening to those around him. His lack of selfishness and quiet deferring manner were markers of the Andrew Daher style. (If Andy had made an enemy in this or any other community, I invite that person to come forward, but intuition tells me that such a figure could only be a fictional character.)

In our racially troubled society where university campuses are no exception, Andy lived his first and last years at Stanford in Ujamaa, the Afro-American Theme Residence. The tendency of our communities is to manage the tensions of race by avoidance. How could I, as a father, be any prouder of my son than to know that at the end of his freshman year, five Afro-American male friends asked him to join their draw group of six in order to live with each other? And how many of us in our constantly mobile culture, where ephemeral relationships often are the norm, have comrades who have been friends for over eleven years, half their lives, laughing and crying through middle school, high school, and through Stanford together, and then choosing to live together as roommates? I nod in deep respect to my son's loyal and loving friends.

In March of 1996 a young man named Jason Karpf was due to be married the next day and went to the roof of the UCSF parking garage to sit and meditate with the stars. He fell to his death and a gathering of family for the wedding became his funeral. I was horrified by the deep tragic theme of this story. One year ago almost to the week, Andy's extended family gathered on this campus to celebrate his graduation. A year later we are here to bury him. Receiving the late night phone call that your child has died is the potential nightmare most parents fear. Judy, her husband Ron, his sister Carrie, and I are now summoned into such a tragedy, as have too many mothers, fathers, and siblings who have lost their children, brothers, and sisters through the violence in our urban neighborhoods, suburban schools, or from the confusing pendulum of illness or accidents. I will strive to honor Andy, as I face this loss of my only son, by taming my own bubbly blood with the intelligence and dignity he evidenced so often through his life. A life that was so short, so sweet.

These words are too brief, too inadequate, but look around you, see how we have come together, feel the love and the

energy that has called us. This ritualistic gathering is the
genuine tribute to Andy. Thank you for this living celebration
of a great kid, my son.

I elicited these remarks from my sorrow and pride two days before
their delivery in the first extended quiet time I found since Andy's
death. Andy never wanted to be in the limelight and could not
have imagined this type of gathering as a response to his life. I, as
the son of a *storyteller,* needed to use my voice to honor him, even
as the hurt and the despairing part of me wanted to flee.

The others who spoke—his friends, Ron, and his mother—
were very engaging. Each depicted their remembrances from the
angle of light that bounced off our son in memory. Andy's friend
Sterling lightened the heavy atmosphere with an address
entitled: "Andrew Daher, Party Animal." The portrayal of Andy in
such a reversal of his assumed image was refreshing, and Sterling
went on to reveal how, in the closing months of their senior year,
Andy had begun to loosen up from some from his ambitious
academic commitments. He eventually even joined his African-
American roommates on the dance floor after some behind-the-
scenes coaching on the precise style of rhythm required. All these
anecdotes were carefully wrapped in the deep affection Sterling
held for his friend. Judy had decided to write a letter in the present
tense to Andy, and the depth of the emotions contained within
it carried most of the mourners to further weeping. We were
educators and could speak, but never would have imagined that our
talents would be required for such a day.

Jerry Drino, my Episcopal priest friend who was one of the
celebrants, now instructed this gathering with a very poignant
message. He explained that the Sioux Indians practiced a rite
of keeping and releasing of a soul. They believed the soul at
death dwelled in a deep and central place in individuals whom the
deceased had influenced. The purpose of this was for the perfecting
of each person whom the deceased had loved. However, the next
step was not to hold onto the memories of life as the deceased
had lived it physically, but to release him into fuller life in oneself,
into the family, into the community, and most importantly to
let the life of this soul go forward.

When the mourners arrived at the church, besides the printed
program, two additional items were given. One was a half piece of

paper titled *Remembering Andy* with the rest blank to be written upon later. The second, a white rose—there were three hundred of them. Jerry instructed the congregation to reflect upon their memories of Andy, write them down, and then be prepared to release them. After this reflective time, the mourners were invited to leave their written words in baskets on the altar and to place their white roses on the casket. The procession of hundreds of persons flowing slowly to his coffin, draping it with roses and turning to the family with handshakes, bows, and tearing eyes, was a testimony to the power of ritual. I was emptied while I was being filled. I was devastated yet being held within sacred space. I feared the road ahead, while still cherishing the son I had lost. The challenge to release Andy was at the heart of my grieving process.

The coffin was turned around to symbolize this letting go, permission for his spirit to move on. This was not dropping my son off to his first day of kindergarten or college, or his starting his own family with a wedding. This goodbye was ultimate finality, at least within the bounds of our material world. Andy was to be cremated. There would be no ceremony at a burial site, so this was the final farewell.

A reception in a spacious courtyard area outside the Faculty Club followed. The cathartic affect of the funeral was clearly apparent in my body language. I laughed and breathed and accepted the energy of those who cared for me without intense pain distracting me. I valued having so many of those I loved gathered in one place, not dwelling for the moment on the *why*. There was food, drink, some letting go. My older brother later shared with me a comment he overheard from two students who had passed the reception without knowing its purpose. They apparently recognized Andy from the posterboard photos in the courtyard and realized that this was his funeral reception. One said to the other, "He was such a quiet guy and touched so many hearts."

THE CIRCLE

In the summer of 1970 Joseph Pieper, the German philosopher, told a small group of us at Mount Savior Monastery that with both ignorance and mystery there is the inability to understand. With the former it is because one is in darkness, while with mystery, there is so much light one cannot see. However, he went on to say, despite such light, one never walks smack into the wall while in mystery, as one might in ignorance.

The closest I have come to experiencing such mystery was the gathering of about twelve friends at my home following the funeral reception. Judy and Ron planned a more formal event for both families and close friends at their home to which I had been invited. I had discerned earlier in the week that these post-funeral hours would be very critical emotionally and chose to be surrounded by those who knew me best. I had suggested to my family that they attend Judy's affair, they had known her family for over twenty-five years, and I was concerned that the level of intensity my gathering could reach might unsettle them. I did regret, though, that my daughter had committed to her mother's event and was not free to be up at my home.

We brought extra chairs into my living room and formed a circle with the existing furniture. This room had graciously hosted retreats for my Stanford office, evening Jungian classes for under-graduates, and, only six months earlier, a circle had been formed for my 50th birthday party. Many of the same people who had celebrated my entry into a second half-century now sat to mourn with me. We had no intended format, but I suggested that we go around and each highlight what aspect of the wake or funeral ritual most touched us. Once such sharing started, I was enveloped within emotions, memories, loss, energy, and affections for those there, a synergy I could not begin to capture in words. We framed moment after moment, which became almost alive through the energy evoked. As I took on the role of facilitator, I also shared my own internal responses.

I wept when I described how at my 50th birthday, after we all spoke about our attachments, I wrapped up the reflections by sharing that I had not chosen to pursue certain options in my life because of the demands of parenting. I had no regrets because putting my children first was how I wanted my universe struc-tured. And now, I felt betrayed by that universe.

Others in the circle shared further. My friend Abel told the circle that his older brother had been killed several years before in their Texas border town. He described how for the next two years his mom sometimes became so disoriented when they were driving in town, she was convinced that a young man who happened to be walking on the street was her lost son. She insisted that they follow him until some detail proved her wrong.

I revealed that each morning I began my day by some stretching and Tai Chi, and then prayed for those for whom I sought protection and healing. The Friday of Andy's death I did not awake in my own home. I was attending a two-day retreat for work at a hotel in Half Moon Bay. My routine had been altered enough that when I arose I did not remember *to do my prayers*. I think the group understood that I was neither experiencing guilt, nor assuming that the tragedy's occurrence hung in the balance of whether I prayed or not, a cause-effect assumption. I was simply describing an event, which to me hinted at the complexity of how the *transcendent, our lives, prayer,* and the *unknown* probably are entangled in patterns as strange as the movements of quarks in quantum physics. I had forgotten occasionally to pray other days without tragedy occurring. Might those around me be more vulnerable if I did not pray? If my niece's belief was correct that Andy was ready to be called, then maybe I played my part in such a design. And yet, all these questions are reductionistic in a reality that does not confine itself to particular human thought, of a particular time, in a particular place. Andy lived that morning and died that night, and there will be no *whys* that are sufficient, or even comforting.

My dear friend Susan disclosed that for her the moment of greatest intensity occurred at the wake when I took her up to the coffin to view Andy's body. "I do not think I would have looked death so directly in the face on my own," she shared with the group.

At a later point in the sharing, my relationship with the children came into focus again. I excused myself from the group and returned momentarily with a letter I had written the kids a year and a half ago after having flown home to be with my folks for Christmas.

Dec. 30, 1997
Dear Carrie and Andy,

As I ran to the lake the day after Christmas, on the very sidewalks I used to stroll to grade school on, I reflected upon my own upbringing in this secure suburb east of Detroit. As a young boy in his early teens, I was very much alone in a variety of ways. My parents have always had the best intentions of caring for their sons, but they neither knew, nor understood how to learn about what I needed, and how isolated I felt. I lived in a world very different from today, where same sex attractions were almost never addressed unless in mean humor or condemnation. With my strong Catholic identity, the foundation for my self-esteem has some significant cracks given what I was exposed to about people who were different.

My urge to share these reflections is not primarily stemming from the above, however, but from the further chain of thoughts that lead me to pondering about my status as a father. For, if I did not get all I needed from my own family as a child (and few of us do, as I can verify in my role as a therapist to young adults), then surely I also have fallen short in giving what my own children have needed for their growth and well-being. Given the reality that you for the most part did not get to grow up in an intact family, there are plenty of areas where your experiences as children did not get validated and cared for in a manner I truly wished could have happened.

I cannot change the past, but I can offer to you the willingness to continue to learn how to be a good father to you as you progress through your twenties and on. Parenting is only partially a natural inborn inclination, and many of the skills need to be learned. I was taught some basic ones from my own parents, but in the area of emotional caretaking, there were some gaps. So, you will need to have the patience and courage to be direct when I miss the mark and you need something different from me in any given moment of disappointment, frustration, or sadness. This does not imply that we will not continue to have differences, and that I will not draw the line and make decisions that you may not agree with or like. However, I want to hear and understand more about when you may not feel understood by me, so that on some Christmas in the future you will not be remembering only the loneliness that is inevitable in each of our lives, but also the love that I deeply experience every day for each of you. . . . Dad

Some of my friends in the circle hardly knew each other, and yet the sharing of loss through ritual bound us in a manner we did not fully understand. My friend Lee, a young psychiatrist who is quite confident in his atheistic paradigm, remarked *that if spirituality indeed existed, this is it*. In Jewish ritual there is the practice of sitting Shiva for a week. A few of my Jewish friends suggested that our ritual reminded them of those dynamics. Never having been part of one, I imagined the parallels between our spontaneous gathering with Andy's symbolic presence to this centuries-old ritual of honoring the deceased.

Perhaps my friend Andy C. from Boston captured the numinous quality of this time best when he later said to me: "I felt it was like being in heaven. . . ." We collectively stumbled down the tunnel and were touched a tiny bit by the white light but were offered no choice to cross over. All of us returned to the world from which we started, my son being the exception.

Time had stopped, though. The phone rang and my older brother indicated that my family was ready to return to the house. I was shocked that five hours had passed.

So, at dusk on the 8th day, the circle was broken, friends dispersed.

ACT II
Players

Photos of Andy, Carrie, and myself.

PROTECTION

Andy at three years of age.

MATCHING STARS

Father and son on summer vacation.

CLEAR-EYED

Carrie and Andy, Christmas photo portrait, 1997.

CRACKING GLASS

Doug and Andy at Palmyra, graduation weekend.

ACT III
Inside

THE CRYING

In my talk at the funeral, I started with this improvised remark: *My family and Andy's friends have cried a river this last week and I am hoping that the river has enough tears to get us through these next moments and give us a little time.*

During the first months after my loss, particular phrases and stories continually emerged when I shared with others. When I was a teenager, my aunt lost her elderly father. She had a spontaneous outburst of tears and mantra of *Pappa is dead, pappa is dead. . .* as we first arrived. When others arrived, her response was identical, but just as spontaneous. Grief reactions can take the form of lines in a tragic play, and we become the actors primed to deliver them over and over again.

The *wheres* and *whens* of my crying were sometimes predictable. I often found myself telling the same two stories about Andy as I lunched or walked or sat at my home with friends and anticipated that I would cry. The first was related to me by one of his roommates, Lexy. Andy had been working long hours and Lexy and Allan were missing his company. Lexy's parents were throwing her a birthday party on a Sunday afternoon, and she had asked Andy to try his best to make it even though he was going to the office to catch up on work. Andy never made it to the party. When Lexy returned to their apartment, she saw his light on and was ready to get angry with him. She found Andy on her bedroom floor assembling a new bed he had bought for her. She hadn't been sleeping well on her old one so he went out and bought this gift to surprise her. That was Andy, choosing to find pleasure in giving to his friend instead of attending a social affair.

The other story I found myself repeating was about a trip to Reno Andy took with a few friends before starting his job. Andy was always a bit energized by gambling. He ended the night $100 up and retired to his hotel room with his friends. While sleeping he had the following dream:

> He went to a blackjack table and told the dealer he was going to play a single hand. He laid his $100 down and was dealt the perfect hand, a black jack and an ace, which pays one and a half times the original bet.

The next morning he woke earlier than his friends and returned to the sparsely populated hotel casino. He laid down his $100 and indeed was dealt a perfect hand. He took his $300 and proceeded to the reception desk where he paid the hotel bill for all of them. I will return to this story later to reflect upon another layer of meaning, a foreshadowing of the ending of his life.

Taking showers often seemed to be a vulnerable time for me that resulted in tears. I looked at myself in the mirror, my distorted face where pain, hopelessness, and sorrow all converged in a portrait of despair. As this routine of crying in various circumstances marked my grieving process, I wondered if these expressions would remain cyclic, me walking in circles of pain, over and over again. Would there eventually be any direction to this expulsion of tears and moans? I knew that crying could be cathartic, helping the psyche and body rid itself of an overload of tension. Such an understanding did little to convince me that my enduring this pattern of endless tears was taking me anywhere.

I reminded myself of an analogy I have shared with my patients, that of climbing up a mountain on a path that circles it. While walking on the path you may see the same sights over and over again, but it does not mean that the trail is not taking you upwards. The period of mourning demands of the grieved intense and repetitive expulsions of pain. If mourning does not occur in a timely fashion, delayed grief can be deeply disruptive in its often disguised emergence at a later time. However, when in the middle of a valley of tears, visions of healing and growth are elusive.

In contrast to predictable tears, there were times when crying caught me by surprise. It had been over two years since Andy's death when I attended a performance of *The Laramie Project* at the Berkeley Repertoire Theatre. Of course, I knew the play was about this town's response to the horrid death of Matthew Sheppard, an exploration of a community's grief and self-examination. What I was not prepared for was a very vivid description from the actual autopsy report of Matthew's fractured skull. The tears began as I flinched in recalling descriptions from my own son's autopsy from his fall.

Then there were the occasions when tears were expected. Andy's birthday is Valentine's Day, which used to be a day of double celebrations for our family. Now, this day would always require a certain emotional preparation in order for my spirits not to plummet. How could there not be tears? I have thrice planned rituals where friends gathered on the day marking Andy's death. Anticipating, honoring, and sharing the deep emotions evoked on such days may multiply the tears involved, but also invited those tears to bathe raw wounds.

THE DESPAIR

I knew from my professional work, and had been warned by a few friends, that the battle for emotional survival begins in earnest as the rituals end. As my friends and relatives returned to their own lives, I was left on my own. The shock to my psychic system began to diminish, and I was pulled toward nonexistence. No energy was available to draw upon, only a moment to moment density of obscure affect and numb plodding through daily tasks. I tried often each day to surrender into the Buddhist perspective that the nature of life is suffering and to not resist being in such a state. What could I do? Flee from myself and the reality of this loss? I went to bed exhausted each night from having carried such emotional density. Sleeping provided welcome respite from my pain.

I decided to take sick leave for the summer and began working on my house. The chance to work with my hands and touch something concrete was a stark contrast to my usual work with elusive psychological dynamics. Physical work had a foreseeable end. There was no laughter in me. I could barely smile. I inhabited a darkness not foreign to me, but one in which I now had been assigned permanent residency. The major task I assigned myself was the repair of my very large redwood deck. Hundreds of 2 x 4s on top of the tar roof of the attached garage were rotting from the bottom. The labor involved prying up each individual board, hammering out the nails, cutting out any dry rot, sanding each down, and coating each with waterproofing. The project filled my nostrils every day with sawdust from the sanding, and after the summer I required several weeks of physical therapy for my strained leg muscles from too many hours of being on my knees pulling and hammering nails. I didn't care. Let the body suffer. It was nothing compared to my psychic pain. When my friend Jimmy visited me from back East a month after Andy's death, we ran in the hills after working on the deck. The end of this run consisted of four continuous small hills that usually challenge my stamina. This time, I was oblivious to any physical discomfort when running them. Physical discomfort was drowned out by the despair.

There also was an underlying numbness and dissociation that seems to protect but keeps the world gray for those who are in deep and continuous grief. Others have described this despair as their world having lost any color. This blandness provided an insulation that protected me from too many environmental demands, but if experienced for too long, it might suffocate me. While watching TV or a movie, my senses were engaged, taking in all the stimuli, the brain processing the information, and yet I remained detached, watching without the will to actually see or care about the seeing. Repetitive routine in a world that was no longer alive, such was the gruel of my despair.

My despair separated me from my parents and brothers while at the same time heightening my connection with my daughter. I did not have the energy to relate to my mother, father, and two brothers in my usual manner. My family had always cared about me a great deal, but differences in our temperaments and sexuality resulted in my often feeling certain parts of me were invisible to them. Consequently, in being with them, I typically held back many of my needs and tried to be the good listener, attentive and supportive.

This was especially the case with my parents. Their long-distance phone calls often consisted of such topics as weather or sports once it was clear that the kids and I were doing well. After Andy's death, they consistently asked about how I was doing, but their ability to listen without becoming anxious was too limited to rely upon. My younger brother has a heart of gold, but his own life challenges required most of his energies. My oldest brother has more capacity to bear intense states and made an effort to not only keep in touch, but also to occasionally send a card with some of his reflections or books he thought might help. Despite the residue of many years of competition between us, these responses hit their mark of support. But my responses to him were muted by depression.

My despair further bound me to my daughter. She called frequently to check in and keep me abreast of her current happenings. She asked about my friends whom she also knew, probably measuring how much contact I was having with others. She had relocated to San Francisco, forgoing her teaching opportunity in Latin America to be nearer to her parents during these dark months. We hiked. I occasionally came up to San Francisco for dinners, and we carried, often unspoken, a void in our hearts, an emptiness Andy was not there to fill. And most clear to me was the utter vulnerability I bore each day of the chance of her being in harm's way.

The consequences of this despair on my own spirituality were apparent to me. Faith was struggling along, but Hope was under deep assault, and I wondered if it had suffered a fatal wound. I faced "the astounding mystery that God's very nature is disclosed in spirit-crushing poverty, among those experiencing deepest loss, at the point where life and sanity are most threatened" (Lane, 1998, p. 78). I did not question whether or not God existed in this desert, but wondered if it made any difference or not. Why remain sane? Why remain at all?

My friend Alan visited me from New York in July, a month after Andy's death. We drove to the ocean one chilly overcast afternoon and walked along the beach. At one point, as he walked ahead of me, I had the urge to just step into the ocean, keep on walking, and not return. Just let the waves tumble me down, end this, be submerged as life's breath is replaced by nature's salty ointment as last rites. I disclosed this imagery of suicide to Alan a few minutes later as I caught up with him. He listened, understood, and asked nothing of me. He let despair have its moment, trusting it would not be my last.

I remembered a quotation I use in one of my class lectures from Arthur Miller's *After the Fall:*

> Quentin, I think it's a mistake to ever look for hope outside of oneself. One day the house smells of fresh bread; the next day of smoke and blood. One day you faint because the gardener cut his finger off; within a week you're climbing over the corpses of children bombed in a subway. What hope can there be if that is so?

I had always looked for Hope outside myself, and that was a dangerous faith to hold. If one was not afraid of death, of possible nonexistence, then the well of Hope needed to be sufficient in order to encourage the despairing not to give up. Faith may give strength to those who shudder when contemplating the future, but Hope is essential to care enough to look forward.

My period of deepest despair occurred about eighteen months after Andy's death. I took an unpaid sabbatical after my return to work for the year after his death. I hoped during this time to reevaluate my present life circumstances, particularly my professional identity. Perhaps in Silicon Valley's booming economy, my creative side could find a niche in the changing world of technology and education. Also, I intended to volunteer my time to community organizations. None of this worked out because I had no energy to sell myself, my knowledge, or my skills to others. My energy was fleeting, ghost-like, undependable. Friends were concerned, and some urged me to consider anti-depressants. I resisted. The despair was so real that it needed to be faced. Yet, I could not promise them or myself that I might not end up paying too high a price. Some friends wanted me to leave my hill, be in the city, be engaged with people. I resisted. A few friends were more patient with the deep angst they observed in me, supporting me, not suggesting I do anything.

A small group that I belonged to was reading William Bridges' *The Way of Transition: Embracing Life's Most Difficult Moments* (2001). In this book, Bridges applied his expertise about organizational change to the loss of his spouse. Having read a previous work of his, I was not so much struck with the content of his ideas, but was very much supported by the clarity of his language about the particular phases in loss. He described a *neutral zone,* a period between letting go of the past and embracing new possibilities for the future. The *doing* of the initial loss period had stopped, and the activity of new beginnings was not yet reality. There was only the void. "It is a colorless streak of emptiness that spreads across your life, like the gray smear left by a dirty eraser" (Bridges, 2001, p. 155). It gave me some patience and resolution to discover that in the deepest despair, when nothing was happening in my life and I did not have the energy to make anything happen, I was exactly where Bridges perceived one needed to be. The importance of honoring *being* over *doing* was philosophically so clear to me given our out-of-balance, action-oriented culture. Still, tolerating the emptiness of *being* month after month was frightening and confusing.

One Saturday evening in February, I lay down on my family room couch, declining to distract myself with reading, TV, or music and just entered into the nothingness. What was left for me? I was not at work, not sure I had the drive to go back to Stanford, was without my professional identity. I had no intimate partner and had not had one for several years. I had lost half of my immediate family. The only concrete anchor I seemed to have outwardly was my home, *Palmyra,* which had offered me in this mourning period a focus for my daily world.

I bought my house in the redwoods during Andy's senior year in high school, while Carrie was a freshman at Brown. Initially, I had hoped for several years to buy a small cabin in the woods, a retreat for soul space on weekends, but the opportunity arose to buy a house in which I could actually live full-time in the woods. After living here about a year, several Jane Austin novels were released as films: *Sense and Sensibility, Persuasion,* and *Pride and Prejudice.* In the middle of watching the third, it dawned on me that all these great English estates had names. I had the sudden urge to name my house and its surrounding acre, and it only took 7/8 of a second to know it would be called *Palmyra.* This is the name of some ancient Roman ruins in the Syrian Desert that I visited in 1986. This landscape had more spiritual impact on me than any other place I have ever been, though I only recognized such an effect years later.

Now, as I lay stripped of almost everything, I knew that to fully surrender to this zone of nothingness, I had to offer up Palmyra. *So be it,* I said to myself. *If the spirit calls me forth to leave even my home in this state of nonidentity, logic be damned, I will.* The following morning, Sunday, I awoke with more energy than I had had for months and took a vigorous walk in the county park near my home. The despair was lifting.

THE ANGER

On several occasions during my life journey, I have looked at myself in the mirror and perceived a man who had evolved, but I still resented what was required by the process. To individuate,[1] for me, means such tension in consciousness that I too often want to abandon ship. Yet, I at times intuitively glimpse the transcendent connection that is a beacon of some purpose, reason for the struggle. But, for how long and at what costs? Yahweh did not take Abraham's son in sacrifice, but here I am being asked to endure this ultimate loss. Why?

Anger is an emotion that is almost always paired with hurt. Most individuals I know seldom have reactions with equal proportions of these emotions. One is usually primary; the other secondary. My pattern is to initially feel anger, but not stay there too long. I get more stuck when I move onto the hurt stage.

I have already discussed my intense anger at my son's employer during the first week after his death. Likewise, in the next section when I share my stories about the ins and outs of dealing with systems, the anger will be very apparent.

There were incidents of unconscious insensitivity by those around me that fried me inside. I was in a meeting with deans at Stanford about six months after Andy's death and student crises were being discussed. A drunken student had fallen off a balcony at his dorm and injured himself. In trying to relieve the tension that reviewing such troubles in long discussions can elicit, some humor was batted around with regards to students falling off buildings. Everyone in the room knew about Andy's death, but in the moment

[1] Individuation is a Jungian term referring to the internal potential in each person to fully evoke into his or her own authentic Self. The Self is understood to be at the core of our being, richer and more whole than our ego awareness.

the parallels did not occur to them. I held my peace, there was no intent to be disrespectful, but I was angry, then hurt. I vented later to a friend.

The larger issue, though, is how angry am I at the existential level when staring into the brutal reality that Andy died? This is a question that confused me. That I am so unclear about where such anger resides within me leads me to suspect that there remains a lot more. There is no one to directly blame for Andy's death. I can shake my fist at the heavens and curse, but I don't, and I am not sure why. My familiarity with suffering, both personally and as a clinician, leaves me more likely to be anxious, despairing, or shut down, but not enraged. Without access to my anger, there may not be the chance to have catharsis. Without recognizing my anger, there is the murkiness of depression. Entering into the anger brings vulnerability. My failure to do so probably offers some armor in the short run, but is not advisable for optimal human contact. He is dead. I need to scream more, but have not done so enough.

In the fairytale *The Frog Prince,* the dilemma for the princess is losing her golden ball down a well. An ugly frog strikes a bargain to retrieve it for the privilege of sleeping in her little bed. She forgets about him once her ball is back in hand, but her father, the King, insists the promise be kept and the frog enters her chambers. She is repulsed, and responds with the brute honesty of her rage by tossing him at the wall. The impact transforms him into the prince that he is, breaking a witch's curse placed upon him.

A friend challenged me to elicit the angry voice inside of myself. To listen to it. I did so:

> I want no part of this hell you call life.
> Giving me an infant to hold, nurture and let free,
> And then, in those moments of release, to snatch him away.
> Who do you think you are?
> One who others address as mighty and powerful.
> I shake my fist at you, as Job should have done from the start,
> And say, I want no part, I refuse to be a player in this game.
> If I am to be so cursed, then curse life itself. . . .

This is a mere scratch on the surface of the existential rage that surely lies beneath. Others may see it in me before I can claim it for myself. I am often just too tired, though, to stay very long in this pit.

THE LONGING

I long to see my son again, to touch him, to smile at his dry wit, and be amazed at his wisdom, despite his being such a young man. I miss the whole range of father-son dynamics. We shared sports, he being a lot more informed and knowledgeable about players and teams than I, but we were equals in our passion for victory. I want the phone to ring again and hear his dry but deeply connected voice saying, *hey, Dad.* I long to casually look up and watch his beauty, to be back in my ignorant belief that there would be so much more to observe and enjoy as years pass.

I regret not seeing more of his playful side. He was so serious, taking out an IRA during his freshman year at college, yet I knew there was the boy inside. During the first work-related conference I attended after moving into the woods, Andy was to be caretaker of Palmyra. I discovered a few cigarette butts on the deck upon my return and assumed that some of Carrie's friends must have been smoking. Only after his death did Carrie reveal to me that Andy had thrown a major party for his high school friends and managed to clean up the place (replacing broken glasses and all) without my knowledge. I am delighted to hear that my overly responsible son had executed such a boyish plan.

Though our personalities were very different, Andy being the introvert and much less emotional than I, our psyches were always in tune with each other's, beyond the realm of probability. Once when he was an early teen, he came across a deck of *Old Maid* cards we played with when he was younger. We sat on my bed and dealt the cards, and thus unfolded an amazing pattern. Each of us ended up placing the Old Maid card in the exact position within a full hand of cards where the other chose it. Try as we would as picker to second guess the location of the Old Maid card and avoid it, for as many as ten hands in a row, that single card was exchanged.

Such a defiance of statistics also occurred the Christmas before his death. Both of us were to fly into Detroit from the Bay Area to visit my folks for the holidays. Carrie would be making her own arrangements from Boston. Because of Andy's unpredictable work schedule and my being on a waiting list to use my frequent flyer miles, I told him to book his flight independently. The only parameters involved were that each of us was to spend about five to six days there, arriving one of the days before Christmas. He had already booked his flight when I decided not to wait any longer for a free seat to open and buy a ticket. Forgetting to check with him about his itinerary, I selected the days for my flights from dozens of choices and from three Bay Area airports from which I am equidistant. When I next talked to him, he reminded me that he had already bought his tickets. Flying separately? Nope. We independently had chosen the same days to fly in and out, the same airport, the same airlines, the same exact flights from a choice of five each day, and the same return itinerary as well. We responded to the world and those around us quite differently, but we viewed it through identical lenses and walked in stride when we were together.

As can be so typical of parents, my pride in Andy was most vocal when I talked with others about him. Be it with friends or colleagues at work, my children were the plums I carried as a reminder of ever growing life in the universe. A psychiatrist friend remarked while looking at a photo portrait of Carrie and Andy how *clear-eyed* they appeared. Ten years before, when Andy was in a Little League playoff game and got a hit, I did a dad-cheer, and the man next to me sweetly commented, "Oh, the proud father."

Of course, Andy was not without his own dark moods, struggling inside himself with all the opposite manifestations of those ideals for which we loved him. On the morning of his funeral, I sat on my front deck at 5:00 A.M., unable to sleep, and was joined by Andy C. who had flown in from Boston the night before. I talked about Andy's moodiness that often occurred when we two were alone and was a compensatory reaction to his keen attentiveness to other people's needs. Andy C. pointed out how much trust Andy must have had in his father to allow his moodiness to emerge in our common time. How true. The boy could brood until late into the morning when we traveled together, and I learned to wait for conversation until his social graces returned. He was not a saint, not often the sinner, but conscious to a fault not to call attention to his own preferences, almost always willing to defer as others met their needs. I long to witness how his generosity could have blossomed as he grew in skill and shared his talents in wider dimensions within the larger community.

A month after his death, when Jimmy had come out from the East coast to help me mourn, we headed up to San Francisco to have dinner. After dinner we had some time to spare and began browsing on the street. In one clothing store, Jimmy saw a CD at the register: *Dance with Angels.* He insisted I must get it, for this music had guided him through his grieving for the sick children for whom he cared through his work at the Hole in the Wall Gang Camp. I bought it. From the first time I heard it, I knew that Janet Jackson's song, "Together Again," would be my mantra song in remembering Andy. Independent of me, Andy's mother started to listen to a half dozen of Andy's CDs after his death. Upon hearing this Janet Jackson song, she knew that the music connected her to Andy. Carrie also discovered in Andy's CD collection an entire Janet Jackson CD with five different versions of just this song.

On a Sunday morning several months later in mid-September, I was walking toward the gathering of several hundred runners for my running club's charity run. Having parked several blocks away, I was privately visiting with my emotions concerning Andy while I hummed this song to myself. As I arrived within range of the large crowd, I realized that loudspeakers were entertaining the stretching runners with music. And, yes, of all the songs known to humanity, the synchronicity of the moment was in tune with my private humming, with Janet's voice herself singing "Together Again" over the loudspeakers. This particular song, through its own energy, became designated in the Daher clan as Andy's memorial song. A few of the most poignant lyrics are:

> There are times when I look above and beyond.
> There are times when I feel your love around me, baby. . .
>
> I dream about us together again . . . what I want is us together again . . . All I know is that we will be together again . . .
>
> Everywhere I go, every smile I see, I know you are there, smiling back at me,
> dancing in moonlight,
> I can see your smile shining down on me . . .

Longing filters the emotions differently depending upon the mode of time I am in. The past brings memories that intensify longing with such sweet sorrow. The present is full of the void of nothingness of that damn neutral zone, and the future whispers of mystery, of such infantile wisdom of hoping for the personal *kairos*[2]: father and son together again.

THE REMEMBERING

There would be no need to face the challenge of moving through the past to the stark present of loss if I did not have the capacity to remember. In grieving, sometimes the memories are solicited, many times just triggered by life's props.

Some of my strongest memories are of the period shortly before Andy's death. The late afternoon before the night he died, I was at a picnic for our health center. In warming up for a softball game with one of our new internists, the ball we were playing catch with sailed over my head and hit our retired physician's two-year-old granddaughter on the head. She ended up not being harmed, mostly just startled, but the look of anger and fear on her grandfather's face in response to the threat of harm remains etched in my memory. I, a parent, recognized that look. None of us knew that such danger for a child would be reenacted within hours with my own son. Unfortunately, in Andy's case, it was not a close call.

The last time I was with Andy was on a Sunday for breakfast, ten days before his death. We discussed a new course on mediation that I was teaching at the university, and then he and I went off to play tennis. He beat me six games to none. I knew I was slowing up, being now over fifty, and was ready to pass the torch. While leaving the tennis court that last morning, he jokingly asked about the beating I had just received, and I replied that it was nothing compared to the beating my heart had taken. I was referring to my own loneliness in life, my being without a partner. The brief but telling look of empathy on his face was so typical of Andy: seldom shooting but usually hitting the mark when he chose to do so.

---

[2] Judaic-Christian concept of the *appointed time*.

Father's Day was two days after his death. In the preceding week, in anticipation of our spending the day together, we discussed by phone a request I had of him. It would be our last conversation. I wanted him to help me rethink my will before I left later that month for my trip to Turkey with his sister. I asked him if he might consider being the will's executor now that he was an adult. His response surprised me, though it was logical and what many might say. He pointed out how emotionally difficult a time that would be for such responsibility. How well I now understand that, son.

A month before his death, I was at a birthday party for a friend. The party was being held in a restaurant that featured a series of games to be played by the guests following dinner. After a long scavenger hunt, we entered an arts and crafts room which had a laminating machine that sealed wallet-sized items in plastic. I pulled out the high school photos of Carrie and Andy that I always have in my wallet and preserved each of them. Now in retrospect, I cannot decide if this act of preservation was a gift from the gods, protecting at least his image from cracks and wear as I carry it close to me. Or a reprimand from life's wise mentor, chiding me for a silly activity based on a misguided belief in permanence.

I lunched with one of Andy's female friends about six months after his death. She was telling me anecdotes about Andy, and I smiled as I recognized myself in several of them. She described his excitement coming home from the supermarket having found his favorite cereals on sale. She told of his advice after she bought a new car that she be sure to wax it at least twice a year to preserve the paint. She even said we walk in an identical manner. I am not a fool and know that had he lived, one of his realizations as he became older would have been to shudder a bit that he was more like his father than he would have preferred. He probably would have wanted to scrape off a few layers of inherited skin. I grieve deeply when I am most aware that I will not see his sons who would have done the same.

One of my fondest memories is dropping him off in the morning at his high school, probably during his freshman year. Perhaps this happened several times, but he leaned over and gave me a goodbye kiss on my cheek, braving any peer reaction toward his expression of affection for me. Displays of emotion were not typical of him, so such a gesture is very prized in my storehouse of memories. It was in the same school driveway that he took his finger and slightly traced it down the right side of my face, parallel to my ear, telling me I was developing wrinkles. It was an honest gesture of feedback that his dad was aging, nothing more, nothing less. He never ended up rebelling, acting out his testosterone in wild acts, but was becoming his own man, keeping his own counsel, while seldom failing to periodically kiss me on the cheek. I regret he did not live long enough to achieve autonomy through his twenties, so that I could have experienced him returning to me at a later age with some of the unabashed directness with which that fourteen-year-old departed from his dad in a school parking lot.

I flash back to him as a toddler, before we moved to California. I had my dream journal on the nightstand next to my bed. I discovered that *someone,* knowing it to be my son, had used a pen to doodle on the cover. I was at first angry, as a non-mellowed-out father of twenty-nine, but was soon comforted by the thought that I could always look at this mark and be reminded of my boy Andy at two years of age. The journal is on the shelf with a dozen others filled with recordings of life's toils and night-time dreams, and I cherish that scribbling.

In the late eighties a group of undergraduate men decided to work on the first men's journal for Stanford and asked me to join them. We spent six months in dialogue, and then put out Volume 1 of a journal that not only included our writings but also a photo of a male from each of our families. I chose one of Andy at three years of age holding a football as large as his torso in both his hands, as he looked a bit bewildered on the front lawn. This photo was placed on a page with two poems by one of the students, entitled, respectively, "To Be a Man" and "What Will Happen." A copy of this journal was distributed to every undergraduate room on campus. Five years later Andy was a freshman himself in one of the dorms, oblivious to the notoriety of his toddler pose from years before. Students now, several years after his death, pass by a tree planted in his honor outside of that same dorm and perhaps even read the plaque, not matching the image of that young toddler with the name of a stranger whom they only know has been remembered by loved ones.

Andy did not have his own car when he was sixteen, though his older sister did. Once she began a job after school, he was without after school transport for a few months. My then partner was buying his first new car: a Jeep Wrangler. Andy came with us to pick it up, for my partner had generously offered to let Andy use it for the twelve weeks until Andy left for the Los Amigos Program in Mexico. We all went to the dealership in my car, and then I followed them as they drove away in this new hunter green machine, Andy surely feeling a rise in status. It was an existential snapshot for me, as I pondered: *It does not get much better than this, and it will not last. . . .*

Remembering is the yeast that allows my grief to rise. Without my memories of the dead, I might not suffer so much. Without my memories of my son, I would be half the father I am, half the man, half the human. If I would have had to hear a prophecy of his death, I might not have endured. Being fated to carry the memory of his life, I grieve, but I endure. And I am learning to celebrate him through remembering.

THE FORGETTING

Life after life. Life before death. How is forgetting related to oblivion? As new memories of recent life fill my consciousness, the recollections of times with my son are bound to dim. There are no new *living* anecdotes to add to memory. What are the consequences of forgetting? What memories of him *will not* be forgotten up to the moment of my own death? Remembering feels more honorable even in its pain, forgetting is horrifying, even as it may contribute to healing in its own quiet manner. The ephemeral quality of life, its impermanence, is that which allows us to cherish memories. A plastic rose that cannot die could never have inspired *The Little Prince*. Yet change means letting go, and for us who grieve that means more loss since letting go may lead to forgetting. There are spaces between Andy's words that had no sound, and I want to remember every subtle line of his face, to remember those silent spaces. And I can't.

There is no bedroom left in the house that is full of his possessions, there are no private shrines I have secretly built to which to retreat. The tree and bench at Stanford are memorials for all of us, but I have not ritualized my visits to them, even on the anniversaries of his death. I go on impulse.

Andy's mother returned very distressed from an eight-hour deposition with lawyers concerning a lawsuit resulting from his death. My daughter told me that her mom was particularly upset because she could not remember all the minute details the opposing lawyer sought about Andy's life. She was forgetting. It is inevitable that as we cherish memories, we not only change them in our minds but also lose access to some of the facts, to memories themselves.

Friends are often surprised by how much I can remember years later about incidents and anecdotal happenings we have shared. Perhaps being a therapist reinforces my tendency to remember life events. But I am also aware that I remember in more detail the hurts and resentments than I do the joys in my life. With regard to Andy, it seems reversed. I have no doubt I have idealized him in selective memory and have let slip away the mundane, disappointing, and frustrating aspects of our joint life experiences. However, I will not forget so easily his darker moods, for as I have explained, I am paradoxically proud that he so routinely could let such moods show in my company. All the small details of his life that I have already forgotten I cannot account for because I can only speculate about their loss. He fades in some degree, even as his role of son is burnt upon my soul.

Now, there are some days that I do not think about him at all and then am hit again with an episode of deep sobbing. I naturally am forgetting some of his story and will not fight the process.

Ultimately, I do not know much. I realize I know even less as I age. I know little about this great divide we assume in our consciousness between life and death. Andy and I may not be as far apart as the loneliness of missing him suggests. The forgetting may have no effect upon the unknown, an unknown that could offer potential access between this father to his son. Rationalists, who lack experiential knowledge of the transcendent, dwell in the reality their senses bring to them and then philosophize. The religious describe post-death encounters through their beliefs and doctrines, which were often originally based on the transcendent experiences of the founders of their religions.

Neither of these perspectives on the polarity of what happens *after death* helped me to clarify what a future connection between

Andy and me might be. Symbols cannot be reduced to linear clarity, and that is why art reveals as it conceals. The osmosis of a presently living father toward his deceased son, or vice versa, is an ultimate mystery whose signs seem beyond even the outback territory of my psyche. Images of the crucifixion as death abound in Christianity, symbols of resurrection are few in comparison. Death is usually an unwanted but not unknown passenger. A transcendent connection to cosmic realms beyond my understanding is a stranger, whom I have not yet had the privilege of welcoming aboard.

THE LOSS

I sit here today, a few months after September 11, 2001, contemplating how to discuss *loss*. I multiply my son's death by more than six thousand. I try to imagine the scenarios across the country of families who are entering into the first weeks of tremendous grief, who are feeling overwhelmed. I know from experience what they are going through and what they will endure in the indefinite future. My son also died at work, in a context related to his building, but in circumstances quite different from a national tragedy. I was afforded the full attention of friends and my community—a luxury that must be divided when so many die at once. I am again overcome with tears of grief, for collective trauma reactivates personal trauma.

The reality of Andy no longer being here is like losing a part of my body. I can't quite grasp its absence, for I've always known where the part was and could never even assume the part would not be there. I previously discussed the role of protector that is so instinctive to us as parents. We respond keenly to threats. When there is no opportunity to respond, because the loss has already occurred, then one is humbled. Our naïve assumptions about our role in the larger cosmos and our limited control over it shrink infinitesimally when loss comes without a chance to respond and protect.

Loss not only requires a constant bumping into a void in the present, but a letting go of images of what could have been:

Sharing in Andy's start of a family with his intimate partner.
Being comforted that his talents and hard work could offer some security to me when I became elderly.

Having companionship when executing the mundane tasks required of house dwellers, those projects that sons reluctantly join their fathers in doing on Saturday afternoons, sacrificing leisure out of love for dad's need for good maintenance of the homestead.

Seeing executed all the lessons of *how to do* I had spontaneously shown him; *Andy using* that large toolkit I gave him the Christmas before his death.

A collage of endless snapshots of life to be, gone with no option of appeal.

My loss is overwhelming, and yet I also have another child. What of those parents who have only one child, and are grieving for the loss of *all* their children, or those who lose more than one child? Are there hints of hubris that underlie decisions to have only one or two children? Are we unconsciously turning our backs on a Nature that has never afforded anyone a guarantee of absolute safety? I also ponder those grieving parents who have lost a child through violence, parents of those who were murdered or killed by the direct negligence of another. I do not have to face the impulse of revenge within myself in this grief, but others do. I am humbled while recalling the deep compassion of Maggie and Reg Green, whose seven-year-old son Nicholas was killed in a robbery attempt while they were traveling in Italy in 1994. They made the decision to donate their son's vital organs right on the spot, and the world was amazed by their gesture of empathy for others in the midst of such a loss. My loss is not unique, and yet it is mine, my responsibility, and my passage into terrible chaos.

If you want to see God laugh, make plans. . . . Well, if holding hopes and visions of future life for my children is the folly of having expectations, I stand *guilty,* and, when feeling worst, *condemned.*

So the challenge is to empty myself in the present moment, be in the void, as spiritual traditions have taught those who search. To bow in the silence of nothing to do or say, and wait to receive. Simone Weil observes: "It is when from the uttermost depths of our being we need a sound which does mean something—when we cry out for an answer and it is not granted—it is then that we touch the silence of God" (Lane, 1998, p. 77).

Can I stretch my bones enough to be so enriched? Carry me to truth, but pray I, let it not be at the expense of my sanity.

"I am lavished with riches made from loss" (Sarton, 1998, p. 77).

THE ATTACHMENT

The phenomena of attachment and isolation are clearly opposite poles on the continuum of our life experiences. The trauma of loss is often the grand interrupter, who can catapult us from the joys of our human connections to the sorrows of being without loved ones.

The circle of friends who gathered after the funeral at my home generated so much intimacy, Andy C. described it as being in heaven. In the midst of my life's greatest loss, my friends and I entered into such deep attachment. Here we have the paradox of life through death: loss bonding me deeper and deeper to others.

I can remember, as a child of five, sitting across from my house on the sidewalk near a sewer cap that had some small round holes for the water to drain. I would lay small stones on the lid and knock these pebbles around to see which ones would vanish by falling through. But I would also occasionally stop and feel, in a manner that was beyond my years, the experience of being alone, utterly alone—the true grit that my later existential readings in college would describe.

My family of origin would offer attachment on multiple levels, offering some shelter from those existential clouds, but they could neither identify nor nurture the lonely adolescent boy who so desperately wanted attachment in ways they could not understand. Two years before Andy's birth, Judy and I started our own family with my daughter Carrie. I was strolling with Carrie as an infant through a park one spring afternoon where a junior high school class was having an outing. In a clump of bushes off to the side, some of the boys were depantsing one of their own in playful revenge. Such an intense wound of loss stabbed me in the gut. I, a twenty-six-year-old father, could only walk by and glance at the roughhousing as my inner fourteen year-old in solitary confinement yearned for impossible escape. Some of me was ready for fatherhood, a core part of me had never had enough of an adolescence. There it was, isolation, even in the midst of my new precious family.

The day Andy was born, I was in the delivery room with Judy as the natural childbirth protocol calls for, and there was some type of concern at the point of delivery which resulted in Nurse Ratchet ordering me to leave the room. There was no way my attachment to my son was to be so compromised during this moment of birth. I appealed to the medical court of appeals in those unenlightened days—the male doctor—who reversed the order. I did remain and I was connected to Andy as he emerged from mother's womb to father's hands.

In August 1984, I was in Detroit with Andy, visiting my parents when Judy called to say she had decided to seek a divorce. At this moment of intense family disruption, I was with my son, attached as ever, as he, age eight, and I, thirty-five, began to imagine what was involved within this pending loss. However, there we were, father and son, facing an unknown but bonded as tightly as ever. I took him to the toy store the next day to pick out any game he might like, knowing we had to counter the fear with some play. He chose *Battleship,* which we played dozens of times over the next several years. The irony of playing a game that involves sinking ships during the transition of divorce never occurred to me then.

Throughout the years as my two children grew, I formed an even wider support network of friends. As a single man, I observed how alive and dynamic attachments are, being stronger and weaker at times, clearer or fuzzier, more comfortable or burdensome. What amazed me, though, about how I related to my son was the lack of such variability. After he went off to college, I would usually let him initiate calls, giving him room for some autonomy. I cannot recall a single instance in the five years after he left the house of picking up the phone and not being emotionally uplifted by hearing my son's voice. During some of those moments I was a very depressed man, feeling almost more darkness than I could endure, yet if I heard my son's voice saying *"Hi Dad,"* I was attached somewhere deeply in this universe and experienced a sense of relief, a momentary surge of energy.

Five months before Andy's death, the two kids and I were in Detroit for Christmas where my father and I had a very heated argument. In my response to him, I erupted with the intensity of a son feeling invisible for too long.[3] Afterwards, Carrie was her typical concerned and nurturing self toward me, but Andy only withdrew into the basement recreation room to spend the late night hours watching sports, as he often did when he visited his grandparents. I was angry that Andy did not reach out to me more, and after our return to California, I considered bringing up this issue with him. But my intuition steered me away from this course of action.

I did, however, start to have the impression that I wouldn't be as much a part of Andy's life once he progressed through his twenties and into his thirties. I felt the attachment was changing. I did not know why, but I sensed that I was not going to have access to him in the same way. I also could never elicit images of Andy physically as a full-bodied adult. That is, I could not imagine his adolescent thinness filling out into a heftier man. In hindsight, I understand that the lack of these images and the premonition of change in the nature of my attachment to him was my psyche trying to prepare me for loss.

A question remains on the table after this intense time of grieving: What is the nature of my attachment to my son now? In disclosing his struggles around the death of his spouse from breast cancer, Bridges has mentioned his worry about how she is faring as she journeys in the afterlife. I am somewhat thrown off by this reference to such a worry because I have always assumed that given who Andy is, he is doing just fine. Andy is using Andy to be a light force. Or is this just the proud father being naïve? Am I neglecting my part in this new attachment by not sending him strength and prayer energy? Or am I following Jerry Drino's reminder to us during the funeral: the casket is turned around on the departure from the church as a sign to let the spirit of the deceased go on and not to hold on even though our grief pleads

---

[3] A half *humorous* anecdote from years before reveals much in this regard. My parents were visiting me in California and staying at my home. I had given them directions to the health center on campus and we were to meet at 6:00 P.M. for dinner. I had finished with my last patient at 5:00 P.M. and decided to change into my gym gear and get a run done before they came. While running along a sidewalk between open fields and a campus road, up pulled my small station wagon that they were using. I assumed that they had seen me. However, my mother rolled down her window as the car pulled over to the curb, saying, *Sir, we need directions.* Only when I came closer did we all laugh, for they had not recognized me, their son.

for us to do so? Remembering–forgetting, what are the proper proportions when loss leads to a transformed attachment? Today we are honoring. Tomorrow do I hand myself over to creatively moving on? I hold precious my deep pleasure in who Andy was, but am I also being called to release the Andy who is, to a wide and mysterious cosmos?

ACT IV
Systems

When struck with the reality of the sudden death of a loved one, self-absorption is almost inevitable. As we are shaped and limited by the loss, grief seems to envelop us during nearly every waking moment. Reverend Jerry Drino explained to me that in the Navajo tradition, when approaching a grieving person one offers neither condolences nor hopes for things to get better, but says in their native tongue, *Something great has happened*. *Great*, not with a valence of something good, but of something large, that will disrupt because of its size. One of the challenges of going out into the secular world while in deep grief is the mismatch between individuals who have had *something great* disrupt them and systems which are operating in their day-to-day routines.

The self-absorption from this unexpected loss led me to feeling very much the *victim*. I do not want to portray myself in such terms, but on several subtle levels of expression I probably had been communicating such. One of my closet friends at work confronted me almost one and a half years after the tragedy and described my behavior during our previous encounter as being very narcissistic. I realized later in weighing his feedback, that yes, I probably was, and how could it be otherwise, as this grief would not let go of me. This type of self-absorbing energy may not serve us well when dealing with institutional responses to death. In a state of being overwhelmed, I am not likely to tolerate well bureaucratic inefficiency and, at times, requirements that seem without justification.

There is also another aspect of being in a victim role that is a challenge: being *the other.* I have in some circumstances experienced and endured being *other* in the community. However, as a white Caucasian male, I am typically responded to as the majority, the central citizen. Ethnic minorities experience daily what it means to be responded to as the *other* when operating outside of their own communities in our larger institutions. The grieving join, without choice, their own minority group and may be novices at the experience of being outside the norm. And systems typically are neither friendly to the exception, nor accommodating to personal pain.

The question might also be asked: Why should the bereaved even attempt to interact with the bureaucratic aspects of systems, particularly in the early stages of grief? In more traditional communities, the extended families or the *tribe* itself steps into the execution of system requirements and the *troubled ones* are not expected to function with their normal energy. In our more individualistic Western culture, we trade such support of the *collective* for a range of freedoms and individual choice. The piper needs to be paid, though, and when there are tragedies with our loved ones, such trade-offs can leave us facing an enormous set of tasks with neither community protection nor our most adaptive personal skills available. In this section, I share the details about my engaging the systems, not because they are important in and of themselves, but rather because they offer a piecemeal map to those who will have to face such a maze. The internal burdens of grief are more than enough weight to bear, but necessary external tasks and moments of decision-making wait nonetheless. Using one's support system and having the time and place to *vent* are essential coping tools.

THE BANK

One of my first tasks in the world of systems after Andy's death was to deposit his last paycheck from his employer into his checking account. After an initial visit to his bank that was thwarted by my not having a death certificate, I returned several days later, having secured a temporary copy as the coroner's investigation was still in progress. I sat at a manager's desk, and was told *No,* I could not deposit his check into his account in its present form given that he was deceased. The manager called the corporate office and instructed me on the proper wording for a reissued check. I called my son's employer from his desk and had them specifically tell their financial official how the check was to be worded. A week or so later I returned to the bank, and there was a different manager on duty. I presented him with the reissued check. He said he had to call the bank's legal department to be advised how to proceed and then informed me they could not accept the check for deposit in its present form, despite the fact it was prepared according to the bank's own instructions.

I retreated into defiance fueled by common sense. I told him I was not leaving the bank until he deposited the money into my son's account. I could thoroughly understand the need for such specific oversight if I was attempting to take money out of the account but was baffled by this resistance to depositing Andy's own paycheck into his own account. The manager relented but warned me that this was the only time that a deposit could be made into this account.

Due to the nature of this transaction, the mangers I was dealing with knew that a death was involved. Our culture as a whole shuns death and does little to prepare most of us for this inevitable part of life's cycle. The persons on the front lines of our institutional systems typically do not know what to say, how to respond to the unspoken heaviness of grief that fills the space and seldom, in my experience, have the authority or initiative to quickly problem-solve and eliminate unnecessary barriers. That being given, the question arises: When do you disclose that the issue you are there to solve involves the death of your child if the circumstances do not require this fact? I did not want to use Andy's tragedy as a means of evoking sympathy in order to manipulate the system toward my needs. Yet, at times, the level of my distress could be better understood if the administrator at least knew why I appeared so discouraged. There are no formulas to guide such decisions about disclosure, and I used my best discernment case by case.

On occasion, I did receive small but touching acts of kindness from those responding to my requests. The receptionist at the dental office where Andy and I were both patients told me there was no charge for the bottle of fluoride I came to pick up a month after his death. I was touched and taken by surprise, and could only respond with a *"thank you."* Similarly, a notary public, whom I had never met, saw the insurance forms I needed stamped, and we briefly discussed her feelings of vulnerability about her own children's safety. She waived her small notary fee, which was of little monetary significance for me, but I received her kindness as a gesture of honoring.

THE WORKER'S COMPENSATION

The system of Worker's Compensation involves a relationship between four parties: an employer, the employee, the state, and an insurance company that manages the policy. The system is intended to provide protection for the worker but also protects the employer. Though my son was only in his first year of employment, his worker's comprehensive benefit was $120,000. I knew literally nothing about these issues until I began to talk with the insurance company representative several weeks after his death. Our concerns were about how to apply this benefit to his only sibling, my daughter Carrie. In our family expectations, Andy was to have played a very critical role in Carrie's life. At the age of ten, she was diagnosed with a genetic eye disease, retinitis pigmentosa. This disease is often recessive, meaning that many families can pass on the gene for generations without it emerging until individuals who each have it mate, and then there is a one-in-four chance for a child to have the disease. The term RP is actually an umbrella category for about forty variations of problems with the retina, but the category generally involves a scarring of the retina that results in partial to full loss of night and peripheral vision. The result is tunnel vision in daylight conditions, with a probability of such patients becoming legally blind over their lifetimes. Since Judy and I were not able to predict when and if Carrie would become fully blind in her adult life or how this would affect her capacity to be able to care for herself economically, we were hoping that her brother's earning power would be a safety net.

Several weeks after Andy's death, while dealing over the phone with a very sympathetic representative of the insurance company handling this workers comp claim, I learned that Carrie's dependency upon Andy had to be documented as having already occurred and that future intent did not count. The representative did indicate that the policy would reimburse the family for the funeral. We could demonstrate through the manner in which our wills were written that the division of our estate between our two children was to be determined by the level of Carrie's health needs—some or all of Andy's portion possibly going to support his sister. However, this written plan or any other evidence of her possible future financial dependency upon her brother was deemed irrelevant by the law. Most, if not all, of the $120,000 benefit was to be returned to the State. The insurance rep disclosed to me that this was the first time in her nineteen years on the job that she had seen the total amount designated as a return. Had Andy been married or had children, this would not be the case. She advised me to secure a lawyer to handle the claim.

Worker's compensation is a specialty area for lawyers, and I knew none. My friend Alan who had walked to the beach with me in July had a relative whom he described as one of the best worker's comp lawyers in Los Angeles, so I gave him a call. He, of course, also knew future intent was not a feasible basis for a claim but after hearing about my children's relationship, judged that a small portion of the $120,000 could be claimed for Carrie. Oh, if it could only have been that straightforward and without anxiety.

The lawyer took over the case and dealt with the insurance company, while also talking with my daughter and sending her the necessary forms. She eventually was sent a very small amount of money, given the total that was allotted in the policy. A year later this claim continued to be entangled in legal issues, much beyond my immediate comprehension. Eventually I came to understand that the District Attorney in San Francisco had been frustrated by a pattern of delays in reporting claims to the State by insurance companies, and she focused on this case to penalize them. My daughter eventually was deposed, with the State not concerned with her settlement amount, but with the insurance company's procedure. A year after that, my daughter received a subpoena from the insurance company wanting the money back, since they also had to pay the State that amount. The Distract Attorney assured me they had no valid claim and the hearing never took place and was dismissed by the judge. Was the claim worth such anguish for my daughter and me? Maybe, but I did my best to shield her from being too burdened by this affair and was grateful myself that the complications were not brought to our attention until more than a year into my grieving. Unfortunately, such was not the case with my own employer, Stanford University.

THE INSURANCE

Interactions around system conflicts are better for all involved when a sense of victimization is not present. Yet, when in the center of loss, one's role is often as *victim,* whether or not by choice. I was only two months into my grieving when the university and I became entangled.

Year after year, November brought open enrollment for my benefit choices as an employee of the University. Stated clearly each time was that once benefit preferences are chosen, they cannot be changed until the following year, with some exceptions for changes in family status. I made few changes each year and always chose the maximum benefit for not only my own life insurance and accidental death/dismemberment but also for the limited amounts that were offered for my children. So year after year I paid a small extra amount to have the kids covered.

Soon after Andy's death, I called the University's Benefits Office to inform them of this tragedy. They began to process the paperwork for the Life and Accidental Death and Dismemberment (AD&D) policies. I felt conflicted to be doing such business in my sorrow, but there was no one else to bring closure to these logistical realities. I talked to the representative on the phone and then went in person to fill out various forms. Because Judy, Ron, and I had had such upsetting experiences with both the Coroner's Office and detective in the handling of Andy's death,

I had asked to see the Director of Benefits in person. I introduced myself and explained the degree to which I had been distressed. I asked that Stanford take good care in handling these claims.

The companies that issued the policies were both from our state. Since the initial death certificate I presented indicated *cause of death still pending*, we had to wait until the police and coroner's reports were completed. The investigations were completed by August, both concluding *accidental death,* neither concluding *indeterminate.* Because the death certificate was changed from *pending* to *accidental*, it had to be sent to the state capital before we could receive a copy. This delayed the process another six weeks. Patience and frustration were constantly battling with each other. Finally, we had the final death certificate, and I submitted it to the Benefits Office.

The life insurance policy was small: only one-fifth the amount of the AD&D, which itself was not large since these payoffs were not for an employee, but rather for a dependent. The claim for the former proceeded right through, and the company indicated that a check was to be issued soon. However, in talking with the AD&D provider on the phone, I was curtly informed that they would be sending out an investigator before any claim would be paid. I asked why the police and coroners' reports were not sufficient. I was told that they always investigated and, on some occasions, discovered conflicting evidence. Feeling very protective of my daughter, I was not pleased that we had to be part of another investigation.

I called Stanford's Director of Benefits to see if he could at least suggest to them that this process not be overly intrusive to my family. He was on vacation for several weeks. They suggested I talk with his new assistant director. We met on a Thursday. She was quite engaging and empathetic and assured me she would look into the matter and be back to me by Monday. She kept her word, but I could tell by the tone of her greeting in that Monday morning call that the news was not good. She informed me that Andy was actually not covered by either policy. Though the University continued to deduct premiums from my paycheck, the eligibility was limited by the dependent being under 18 or being a full-time student. Andy had graduated the year before his death. Of course, "the University would reimburse me for any premiums I had paid since his graduation" I was told.

I was very upset, and felt more the victim than I had with any other system issue up to this point. I challenged her by saying there was no indication of these eligibility requirements that I had ever read in the yearly open enrollment forms. Correct, but she countered that this was indicated in benefit booklets sent to us every few years. How could they have been collecting premiums from me for coverage that did not exist? She answered that the University could not possibly keep track of the student status of all employees' dependents. I informed her that they had such information right in their office since Stanford has a tuition support program for all such dependents who are in college and monitors their status. She paused and then said their computer systems were not set up to cross-reference such data. *Well, they sure in the hell should be,* I felt like screaming but did not. We ended this quite awkward conversation by agreeing that she would take up the matter with the director upon his return. As a last point, she requested that I return the life insurance check that had been issued and was on its way. Indeed, it awaited me in my mailbox at home that very afternoon.

I wallowed in this one a bit with my colleagues at Stanford and my friends. A perfect victim story. The director had to take the issue up with superiors and eventually they offered a tax-free payment of about one-sixth of the amount due from both policies. I replied that this was not acceptable, and he said that I could write a letter of appeal, but he was not optimistic that the offer would change. He indicated that Stanford's offer was not legally required of them. I was not touched. Eventually, after having written a letter of appeal suggesting that both the University and I were culpable for the situation and therefore we each bear fifty percent of the responsibility, they did offer half the amount of both policies. I was not sharp enough to catch in their document of agreement that they did not offer the money tax-free as the insurance money or their original offer would have been. So, the payment finally arrived in a smaller sum after taxes, having been issued as a supplement to my income at Stanford. It was a significant emotional challenge to confront my place of work for the last twenty years, while in such an emotionally vulnerable state.

THE PREAMBLE

I arrived at Stanford in the fall of 1980, a young professional four years out of his Ph.D. program with a stint at the University of Rhode Island under my belt. People work very hard at Stanford, and the environment is so beautiful that even if one senses burnout, exiting is a difficult choice for many. The fall of 1997 was to be the start of my eighteenth year. As I have earlier indicated, if we had crystal balls of our short-term future, I am not sure I could have arrived that autumn quarter to face what waited, which would eventually end with Andy's death. There were two sets of issues that developed through the year that complicated a depression I was already falling into from too many continual years of clinical work without a significant break.

One issue revolved around the men's group I had run for students the last fourteen years, and the second was my attempt to find a way to take a partially-paid sabbatical year. The combination of these two resulted in a complex set of dynamics that not only drained me but also resulted in a significant amount of conflict between my boss and me. We had, up till then, worked closely with each other. Peer staff members were also affected—many supporting me, a few distancing themselves or staying neutral—and my resentment grew toward the place of work to which I had dedicated so many years of professional and personal effort. I had come to Stanford having convinced myself that one should never have expectations of institutions, for organizations do not have emotions and will not be able to reciprocate commitment and dedication. However, like small ants, expectations sneak in and reappear despite our best efforts to eradicate them. By the spring quarter, I was talking to my boss only when professionally necessary and began searching for a possible alternative source of income to sustain me if I took a leave for several months to a year.

When word spread of my son's death, I was faced with accepting help and kindness from some peers with whom I had remained in conflict. And upon my return in September three months later, the unresolved aspects of these themes remained a source of pain. Eventual mediation between my boss and me helped bring some level of closure to the tensions, but it was not until after my year of leave that the signs of healing between my workplace and me became more apparent. My grief both complicated and intensified the already disturbed circumstance while also humbling me to be more forgiving of those whom I perceived to have treated me unfairly. The juxtaposition of a dean and a director not able to find a way to provide a partial paid leave for me after my long commitment of employment with their paying for the catering at my son's memorial service was confusing. But life, and particularly the mourning period, typically lacks clarity and consistency. A lesson I am learning in my fifties is that if my vision of life's challenges is too clear, I know I am seeing them too exclusively from my own biases. Life dilemmas can be both complex and simple simultaneously, but they are usually always best approached in their symbolic fullness rather than reduced to linear truisms.

THE LAWSUIT

Litigation. The word evokes a whirlpool of responses, internally and in those around us. Fear, greed, retribution, fairness, correction, hostilities, resources. . . .

In the first forty-eight hours after Andy's death, there was the confusion of *whys* and the contradictions between what we knew of him and apparently did not know about him. The questions around responsibility shifted significantly with the anger and shock I experienced when I walked onto the patio area where he died. After that point, there was no keeping the question from being on the table: Will we sue?

Some colleagues perceived that time was of the essence. We were advised to be aggressive about getting photos of the accident area before it was changed and to be very careful about interpreting how Andy's company responded to us. In retrospect, this advice seemed out of context given the regulations and laws that govern the process. The most significant revelation early on was that Andy's employer could not be sued. His death occurred while he was on the job and therefore the employer was protected by the Worker's Compensation laws. Monetary redress needed to be sought through Worker's Comp, but as explained earlier, we were in a catch-22 because our family, and in particular Carrie, was not under *dependent* status. If the firm owned the building Andy worked in, there would be no option for a lawsuit. Circumstances were such that they did not own the building, but rather leased it from a company that both owned and managed the property. The question of liability therefore could be pursued in the courts.

During those next two months, I had numerous conversations with friends about the wisdom, or lack thereof, of pursuing a lawsuit. Some warned that the grieving process is intense enough and that partaking in a lawsuit would only prevent closure and drag the process on for years. A divergent viewpoint was that a suit would be an appropriate focus for my anger, given that there appeared to be negligence both in the manner in which the roof area was built and the creation of a patio area. I was told such lawsuits were the catalyst for corrective change. Others pointed out that if I did not pursue the initial option to sue, I might regret it later on when the statute of limitation had passed. My friend Susan, who had given birth to premature twin sons eighteen years earlier, had faced a similar choice. There were complications following the birth. Susan and her husband were under great stress concerning the newborn twins and their ongoing health issues and had decided against suing their obstetrician for negligence in not attending to problems during the pregnancy. She, in retrospect, regretted their decision not to sue.

There was the expected tension of opposites warring in my psyche: greed, guilt from *profiting* from my son's death, the level of involvement that would be required, the wisdom of letting go, the question of forgiveness, the warning to not be too idealistic, and the expectation of accountability from others. The importance of being patient as the contradictions collided was the bread and butter of what I often offered my own patients. However, my tolerance for ambiguity was wearing down, and I begin to fundamentally question the relationship between money and loss.

When studying theology as an undergraduate, I was introduced to the spiritual challenge of *how to be in the world, but not of the world*. This juxtaposition always has had an intuitive ring for me. There is danger to my soul in being defined by secularism, but I am partially a product of a secular culture—it is the environment in which I live. Money can provide opportunity and apparent security during the journey, but the evolution of becoming fully who I am is not economically based. Why then, in the wake of the grief of losing one's child, would I pursue a lawsuit for money, even if justified on the basis of negligence? Money might provide time for my daughter and me to step away from the constant pressure of the every day world. Compensation could neither lessen nor make more palpable a loss of this depth. However, monetary settlement might offer the option to carry the loss at a slower pace, to breathe more deeply when entering its dark caverns—time to allow not only further reflection on loss, but also an ability to more fully grasp what might be expected when insights are gained.

As late August approached, I reached a decision. In thinking about where I might be with my grieving in several years, I did not imagine that I would have *moved on*. Andy was too central to my life. I might be grieving differently, but I was intuitively sure I would not have closure. Finding a solution to another worry I had about the process also tipped the balance for me. I was dreading the turmoil that a lawsuit would inevitably generate between Judy and me. I could envision the rather intense situation that might arise if a monetary offer was made before a trial and we had to make a joint decision but differed greatly in our choice of whether to accept it or not. I decided to seek representation on my own.

I talked with Judy one evening. I asked her where she was in her decision-making. She said she was leaning about eighty percent against a lawsuit. I told her I had decided to pursue the case. She said, as I knew she would, that if I did so she also had to, explaining that she could not sit on the sidelines with a case in progress. I indicated that I also had made the decision to pursue separate counsel. On that evening, we committed ourselves to a process quite foreign to any prior experiences.

Michael, a younger lawyer, did not present himself with any aggressive edge. He was my man, despite the assumed lay *truism* that aggressiveness gets the best results in litigation. He had a sense of perspective and a sense of internal morality. And, a factor that in my grief process ended up being very important to me: he was accessible. I sometimes wondered why my lawyer was often *in* when I called, which was never the case with the Worker's Comp one, and a small doubt arose that he was not very busy because he was not very successful at his trade. None of my impressions of Michael supported this doubt, and my trust in his judgment and decency only grew as he prepared the case in conjunction with Judy's lawyers.

The depositions did not start until a year and a half after Andy's death. The depositions were meetings where one side questioned an individual in the case for fact-gathering and to get a sense of who they were going to be dealing with if the case went to mediation and then possibly on to trial. During my first attendance at one of the depositions before my own, our lawyers deposed the Vice President of the firm that owned and managed the building where Andy had died. My presence was optional, but I wanted to hear about why the patio was built as it was. We knew that OSHA, having inspected the area after my son's death, had already fined the firm and the management firm for safety violations. However, this evidence could not be used in court because the government does not want correction of unsafe conditions to be used as an admission of guilt in pending litigations which could thereby delay safety changes.

What eventually emerged from a number of depositions of engineers and various managers of the property was that the area where Andy fell had been changed the year before his death due to re-tarring of the roof. The lack of a barrier of sufficient height around the perimeter probably was thought not to be as much of a risk factor at the time of original construction because large wooden planter boxes had been placed there that formed a wall around the roof's edge. These boxes were an inherent barrier, drawn on the original blueprints, and intended to be put back after the re-roofing was completed. Somewhere along the line, the decision was made not to replace these large planter boxes after the re-roofing because it was assumed that their moisture may have contributed to the roof's maintenance problems, thereby leaving the roof without a barrier.

Probably the most potent set of facts for our case was that the city's building department never issued a permit for the re-roofing project and that the area was never inspected by the city and signed off on when finished. Had such plans been submitted and the area inspected, the lack of a barrier and the risk it posed would have been apparent to officials. This perspective was reinforced in consideration of codes for new construction that required a wall barrier of a minimum of forty-two inches. I cannot dismiss the conclusion that if those barriers had been in place, my son would be alive today. Such a conclusion feels too definitive when contrasted to my intuitive understanding of the spiritual realms that highly influence our lives, but nevertheless, is not unfounded. I knew the world of litigation would be narrowed by linear logic and would use a more reductionistic paradigm than mine tends to be. I was angry that our human failings in judgment could have resulted in a young man falling to his death, even as I knew life is never so simple as *cause and effect.*

My own experience of being deposed was not particularly emotional for me. It lasted about five hours, much of the time focused on routine facts about my life, professional work, and, of course, my relationship with Andy. The only source of frustration for me with the opposing lawyer was his constant hammering away about why I did not know more details about my son's interpersonal and romantic life. My replies were mini-lectures about adolescent development and the notion of separation and independence during late adolescence and the college years, much to the chagrin of my lawyer. What did leave an impression upon me, though, was who was representing the other side. The firm had sent one of its seasoned veterans, a man in his sixties, who had decades of experience behind him. He came across very even, probably unflappable, and would be a formidable opponent. Michael pointed out that this was an indication that this lawsuit was being taken quite seriously by the insurance companies. By the following summer, two years after Andy's death, as depositions dragged on, we had a court date set for December 2001.

Mediation, the step before a decision to go to court, awaited us in the first week of August. Michael, on at least two occasions, had tutored me on the legal limitations of a wrongful death suit brought by the family of origin. Since as working parents we were not financially dependent upon Andy, the typical projections of future earnings were not relevant to the case. Likewise, *pain or suffering* and *grief and sorrow of the heirs* are factors not allowed consideration. The grounds had to be on other emotional factors, defined in California as: *reasonable compensation for the loss of love, companionship, comfort, affection, society, solace, or moral support.* The dilemma, of course, was that Andy's role in our lives could never be measured in quantifiable terms, and yet here we were being asked to work only within such dimensions.

I brought up to Michael my son's and my plans to eventually transfer a portion of my home to him each year, so the kids would have the option of keeping Palmyra in the family and not have to sell it to pay taxes. Not relevant. I pointed out that Andy may have played a future role in my elder years of caring for me on a number of dimensions. Not relevant. Most important to us was his possible care-taking role for his sister. Perhaps that could be let in through the side door, he indicated. The subject of how much money to ask for in our demand did not come up once in the two years I worked with Michael, but now before mediation we had to decide.

Michael had been conferring with Judy's lawyers on the issue of *how much* and sent me a letter with the tentative demand amount. A meeting was planned between Michael and me before it was to be finalized. I had the weekend to ponder the amount. Michael's strategy was to go into mediation with a higher amount than we expected to settle upon, but not so high as to have the other side shut down completely. The figure our lawyers suggested seemed low to me. It was not a random figure, but was based upon figures from other cases in the county that were deemed comparable (I was told this would be part of the judge's instructions to the jury if it should go to court). Part of the problem in this process was that the settlement figures that we as lay people hear about are typically through stories in the general media, and these tend to be ones involving high figures.

I detached myself from the world of legal precedent during the weekend, became more receptive to my own intuitive feeling, and asked a few friends for their thoughts. I was determined to go into the mediation process with a focus that I would not be distracted from and not be intimidated by the possibility of having to go to court.

I told Michael in our meeting that I wanted the amount of the suit to be raised. I did not know how he would react to this approach, but his first question was: Have you been talking with Judy and Ron over the weekend? I had not. They also independently had come up with a similar figure. Michael was fine with starting with this figure, though I could read him: this was more fantasy than probable, *the homerun with two outs in the bottom of the ninth*, but nevertheless, it was possible. Juries are unpredictable, but in mediation Michael had a better sense of the upper boundaries the other side would tolerate, particularly given the precedents set by similar cases. Both Michael and I agreed that with this monetary demand, we would not likely reach an agreement in mediation.

The day of mediation ended with Michael saying to me that this was the roughest mediation in which he had ever been involved in his legal career. Since mediation required a confidential agreement to be signed, I am not at liberty to give the details of what was discussed, put on the table, or rejected. After the first forty-five minutes, we were never in the room with the opposing side, which consisted of the management firm's original lawyers and four other lawyers or representatives from two major insurance companies. The mediator moved back and forth between the two groups. Their tactics around time availability were manipulative. The use of the suicide card by the other side was expected, but we did not anticipate it being used so continually with no evidence to support this conclusion.

Since that Sunday two years ago, after first viewing the sight of Andy's death, I had not been bothered by the question of suicide. After the day of mediation, I once again had to search my mind and heart to ask about suicide being a possibility. Both the police and the coroner's reports concluded accidental death, not suicide, but were not admissible in this civil suit if it were to go to court. After two days of soul searching, I received a long voicemail message from Michael summarizing his consultation with Dr. Jerome Motto, the grandfather of suicide studies in the Bay Area, whom we had retained as an expert witness if needed. As Michael reviewed point-by-point how Andy's death did not fit a suicide profile, I reaffirmed my own clinical knowledge that had helped me reach that conclusion, as well as my own intuition. However, self-deception could be clever, and raising this question again was not inappropriate. Michael's message was timely and helped settle me.

The mediation ended with an offer that was twenty-five percent lower than the absolute minimum our side had finally agreed upon to prevent going to court. I noted silently that the amount was exactly what Michael had predicted hours before. The mediator said he would contact us within a week to tell us if the other side received approval for offering this amount and to see if we would accept the offer. Even though Judy and I could independently accept or reject the offer, the reality was that if one of us rejected it, the companies would not settle with the other party because court costs could not be avoided. Judy and Ron left to consult with her lawyers later in the week, while Michael and I had an interesting chat on a street corner in San Francisco.

We spoke a bit philosophically about life and the unexpected. We eventually discussed the pros and cons of accepting the offer if it were approved. My resolve about being quite willing to go to court had been shaken by the nine grueling hours of mediation. My willingness to hear a jury conclude that the case did not hold merit diminished. My awareness that in the case of a no award verdict, I would still be responsible for a portion of thousands of dollars of legal costs was sobering. I knew that the other side wanted to achieve exactly this manipulation of my disposition, and they were pros!

At this point, friends and I discussed what a trial would cost me emotionally. I knew that not settling did not mean a trial was inevitable, and that at any time before our court date, the companies might make another offer. Additionally, the judge would probably attempt to do some mediation in chambers before a trial began. I tried to understand what meaning this money had to me. My daughter and I had already decided that any money I received from the case would be directed toward the long-term future of our home, Palmyra, and the option of creating time for reflection. I also carried with me the irony that Andy always had been the shrewd businessperson in the family, interested personally and career-wise in investments. Carrie has always been more present-focused in her lifestyle, not projecting so much into the future and having more fluidity around money. And now, in this black comedy, I faced decisions about money stemming from the absence of any economic future for Andy and the presence of future economic needs on the part of my risk-taking daughter and myself.

Michael was leaving on vacation with his family the next day and gave me his cell phone number in case an offer was made. Nine days later while I was at work on a Friday afternoon, I received a frantic phone call from Michael's assistant that the mediator had the offer and that it had to be accepted by day's end but she could not reach Michael. Michael and I had already agreed by phone a few days into his vacation about the numbers and he even graciously and generously offered to reduce his contingency a few points in order for me to exit emotionally with a clearer feeling of closure. The bottom line for Michael was not exclusively money. I told his assistant to accept the offer.

As I had been warned would happen, the insurance companies dragged their feet in dealing with the paperwork and cutting the checks for us. After two weeks of waiting, I called Michael once again and asked him to put some pressure on the system. I had awoken in the middle of the previous night with an uneasy feeling of dread, feeling that it was important to get finished with this money business. He was able to get them to sign off on the final documents that day, and we were told the checks had been cut and mailed. Two days later, a symbol of the economic center of the world collapsed on September 11th.

ACT V

The Rituals

TREE PLANTING

The rituals that have honored Andy's death have been essential pieces of my grieving process. The wake, funeral, and circle of friends that I've described were central to my sanity in that first seven days. Since Andy had been his generous self while at Stanford, the University knew him from his volunteer efforts, and it was supportive of a tree being placed in his honor outside of his former residence hall. My daughter Carrie spearheaded the project, and along with the Stanford professionals with whom she worked, she was very committed to creating this symbol for our family.

Ten months later we gathered for the tree-planting ceremony. We decided to limit the invited guests to our friends who actually knew Andy personally and, of course, his friends in the area. There were about thirty guests on a very warm Sunday morning in a courtyard soothed by spring fragrances. A young Washington Hawthorne tree had been planted a few weeks earlier in a recess outside of Ujamaa. A beautiful plaque lay in the ground with his name and dates of birth and death. Also, a wooden bench with his name on a plate was nearby where those passing could rest. Andy's company graciously donated the funds to establish this memorial. I am particularly grateful for an actual physical location since Andy's cremation meant no burial site.

His mother welcomed our friends. After a small prayer blessing the tree, I began the story behind why Janet Jackson's "Together Again" is our family's song for Andy. Then I shared how some of my mornings begin:

> These last nine months have brought incredibly tough challenges for many of us as we try to endure, figure out and respect how to grieve the loss of Andy in our lives. In my morning routine, after finishing Tai Chi and before shaving, I typically say a prayer of protection for those I love dearly. Sometimes I still mistakenly include Andy's name, and with such a mistake I am reminded that the memory of the heart is dominant over the logic of intent.

Such mistakes are typical in grieving, as notions of *before and after* are not necessarily how we relate to the world.

I described the isolation of grieving, especially as the weeks turned into months, thanking those present for their support and, in particular, my daughter. *I know of no better fellow traveler down this very sad path than my daughter.* How could I sufficiently honor Carrie for her consistent calls to check up on how her dad was doing? Her tending to me was not only love felt, but also love executed.

I then shared an observation I had made recently:

> During spring break two weeks ago, I was up at Palmyra, my home, working outdoors. Though I have lived there for six years and cherish being among some thirty redwoods on the land, I did not know until soon after Andy's death that I actually have three separate sacred circles of redwoods. A redwood sacred circle, I learned, evolves in this manner: an initial redwood grows alone in a spot and drops its seeds over hundreds of years in a circle pattern around itself. Eventually it dies and disappears, and the next generation of trees grows and forms a large circle around where the original tree lived. When the sun is at the highest point of the day, the light will funnel down into the center of that circle— which the Indians considered sacred. What I saw and began to ponder two weeks ago is that sometimes a younger new redwood will begin to grow in the sacred circle itself but is

not likely to have the exposure to the needed elements to grow to its fullest size and live hundreds of years. The privilege of being born in the center of a sacred circle also comes with the destiny of life ending at a young age. I am pondering these images, without the need to slip into Hallmarkish sentimentality.

I told the story of Andy at the casino and the perfect blackjack hand. I had shared this with Dr. John Beebe, a Jungian colleague of mine. John understood Andy's being dealt such a hand as a symbolic indication that Andy's present life was complete.

I concluded my talk during this precious ritual by pointing out that perhaps not all redwoods have to grow to full statue and tower for hundreds of years to fulfill their roles. . . .

We turned on "Together Again," wept, and formed a circle: ritual in full life force.

ASHES

In late August, Carrie and I, having canceled our trip to Turkey scheduled a week after Andy's death, instead took a drive up to Vancouver, Canada. Our hearts were heavy, but a retreat from the familiar was called for. Walking in the city during the afternoon, we came upon a shop with African imports, and I examined a black-and-gray ceramic bowl and its cover, which I instinctively sensed Andy might have liked. I bought it with the intention of taking the portion of ashes I was given from the cremation out of the cardboard box and sealing them in this piece of art. In making this transfer upon my return to Palmyra, I held back a small portion with the intention of spreading them in a ceremony marking the first anniversary of Andy's death. That day fell on a Sunday, and I invited several of my closest friends and Andy's roommates Alan and Lexy to Palmyra for an ash spreading ritual and a meal. My reflections in the weeks prior to the event and subsequent remarks came from significantly different moods and vantage points than those of the two earlier talks I had shared. A rendition of most of these thoughts follows:

REMARKS FOR THE SPREADING OF
ANDREW DAHER'S ASHES
June 18, 2000
First Anniversary of His Death

Remembering through the genre of ashes is basic *truth,* with neither the protection of photographically spurred memories nor the poetry of imagined angelic realms where souls may venture.

The concentrated vitality of my only son can hardly be symbolized by these less than featherweight ashes momentarily floating trough invisible air pocket mazes until each finds a minute landing pad of redwood soil within which to merge and lose its chemical identity.

Yet, Milan Kundera fascinated us a decade ago with his book, *The Unbearable Lightness of Being,* challenging us to separate from our normal association of the heaviness of life's journeying and ponder "existence" as light as are these ashes which we will soon be scattering. Light in weight; nevertheless, at times unbearable.

Standing on the slopes of Palmyra, I will share some ideas about *listening* on this one-year anniversary of Andy's death, within the circle of loved ones, and ask you to honor my remarks with the privacy we reserve for such intimacies. At Andy's wake, funeral, and tree memorial, the remarkableness of this young man was celebrated in a range of stories and reflections. With ashes in hand, I am going to reflect in ways which are contradictory to the sense of a destined death I pondered in my April remarks at his tree memorial. Such inconsistency honors the complexities of this last year, for, as when light bounces off of a fine gem, there are many angles of the stone it can catch. *Inattentiveness,* particularly in regards to our own unconscious messages, has been the emerging theme as I prepared for this important day.

Andy was born ugly, can't say it any other way. In contrast to his sister, whose first day photograph portrayed a doll-like quality, Andy's face was wrinkled like a prune. I said to Judy: "Hopefully he will have brains to compensate for the looks." Of course, you all are only too familiar with the results of the metamorphosis that soon took place. Oh, how many girls and women remarked to me about those eyelashes throughout the years. . . .

Andy did not have a bowel movement his first five days of life, much in contrast to his earlier sibling, and the pediatrician assured me in a phone consultation that this too shall pass. . . . Yet how indicative of the child/man to be, contained and careful. . . .

Learning the skill of riding a bike without training wheels, the next sacred childhood ritualistic trauma after circumcision, Andrew achieved without strife and fear. Yet this was not the realm of his inattentiveness. . . .

His grandfather and father were not bad-looking either, but underneath such masculine stature was a cross-generation wound, deep and in need of much attention. I cannot provide you with an explicit analysis of this wound, or even a description, and might not, even if I could. Suffice it to say that this very human wound has not been healed, and maybe at best can be only integrated and not healed.

I have been told by a scholar of Renaissance astrology that Andrew's and my birth charts are *uncanny* in the way they match. He has almost never seen such similarities, statistically off the charts. And so he inherited the wound as have I myself. I now have more language to try to explain why, despite the mother/infant biological realities, my connection with my son is as strong and probably more complex than the wonders of human gestation.

In the summer after returning from his junior year at the London School of Economics, Andy with little enthusiasm offered to help me paint the trim on the front roof of the house. He would paint part of the red trim while sitting on the flat roof, and I would move the ladder along with him as he handed me dipped brushes. Because some of the evergreens blocked the spot from which I would have typically angled the ladder, I placed it with the base further from the house than would have been ideal. I fell as the top of the ladder suddenly crashed forward, with my son watching from the roof. He was calm, somewhat unexpressive, and in a way I couldn't understand at that time, inattentive in a manner that I also was modeling for him. I got up, a bit bruised on my legs, set that ladder up, and climbed right back on it, downplaying the reality that such a fall could have easily led to paralysis or other serious injury. My son saw my courage; he also saw my blind side . . . inattentiveness to what I was being told. Two weeks later, I am embarrassed to report, the same scenario repeated itself a hundred feet down from the previous spot. Andy asked me how I could get right back on the ladder after such a fall. I don't know what I said, but I truly believed I was teaching him a lesson in perseverance. In my masculine strength, I went right back up. I did talk with him a week later about my reflections on the danger and the need to secure ladders differently in the future (which I have religiously done). What he probably did not recognize was this: that I was listening to my inner life, to hear what my unconscious was trying to say: *we are not immune from falling.*

Andy, during his summer in Mexico digging latrines with the Los Amigos Program, was bitten by a dog when he was a few days from coming home, much like his grandfather was as a boy. One of Andy's rewards for a summer of labor for others was a set of rabies shots upon return, and I remember how painful it was for me as a father to watch. Yet, this is not exactly the type of inattentiveness I address.

In the last several months of Andy's life, he was feeling neither the energy nor confidence in his work performance that he expected of himself. Physically, he was constantly tired, and I think he was confused about what this shift in stamina and concentration meant. I talked with him about using my physician as his primary doctor for his HMO choice so he could get a physical. I suggested the option of therapy to review his life priorities. I threw out the idea of his taking the next year off and traveling in Europe to re-evaluate his career focus. But I knew he would not act upon any of this, with maybe the exception of the physical. And this is my point: Andy was inattentive to what his unconscious was trying to signal to him. And I was inattentive to the deeper stirrings of my concern inside. Carrie, her inherited genes *blessing* her with a body that so often has aches, pains, the flu, and of course, a struggling pair of eyes, is learning well the importance of *attentiveness.* How terrible a taskmaster the Wise Cosmic Shaman can be when teaching what we need to learn.

The night before Andy's death I was at a retreat dinner with several administrators from my work. The Associate Director sitting to my right asked how Andy was doing. Without hesitation I said I was worried about him and went on to explain the hours he was spending at the firm and my concern that he was being overworked. Again, I knew more than I was attending to. . . .

Andy, like both his grandfathers, was to be a man of business, and he had what it took to be a rising star. The criteria the strategic business players of the world would have judged him by do not typically take into account the whisperings or rumblings of the unconscious. Andy was wise beyond his years, but wisdom is not the same as integration of our *otherness,* the stuff the ego does not warm up to easily. I don't know if Andy had learned to be more attentive, whether he would have sensed the edge was too near. I just don't know. I do know from my experience, though, that a predictable consequence of doing inner work is seeing all too often how close to the edge we are and praying for the strength not to fall off.

I have shared these difficult reflections because I want this occasion of spreading Andy's ashes not only to be moments of remembering and honoring him but also to remind and challenge us to be attentive to our souls' language. I tire so often of doing it, but the stakes are high if we are not vigilant.

I cannot end, though, without telling another heartfelt story related to Andy. Beyond the question of Andy's degree of attentiveness, we all know that his life energy spoke louder than his use of words. One day last October, Maria, our Student Health Center cleaning attendant for many years, asked to have a few minutes with me. She, like the rest of the Center's staff, had attended Andy's funeral in June. Maria had never formally met Andy but saw him on a few occasions when he was over at my work visiting me. She said she was touched by his presence in some unspoken way. One of her own daughters, she told me, had been dating a Black man for quite a while, and Maria could not accept this Hispanic-Afro-American relationship. After Andy's funeral, she said her heart opened up in a manner she didn't know it could to embrace this man and her daughter as a couple. Without speaking a word, Andy was working his magic—a magic whose source, whether he was attentive to or not, left many who met him with a little more capacity to love.

After I finished speaking and with about ten of Andy's old baseball caps on hand, I asked each person to choose one, put some ashes in, and spread them first within my largest sacred circle of redwoods at the back of Palmyra where we were seated. We walked in solitary paths during this first spreading, and then made our way to the second circle that was in the front of Palmyra to share any last words and finish spreading the remaining ashes. Carrie did not arrive, nor did Alan and Carole. I was concerned that maybe my remarks had upset Carrie or possibly Alan, but this was not the case. Carrie had been overcome by the sorrow the ritual had elicited and needed some extra time to cry, and the two others were attending to her.

When they arrived at the front of Palmyra, others shared one by one, and Carrie spoke quite eloquently about the importance of recognizing first anniversaries of death. She told how Latin and Mediterranean cultures highly valued the significance of completing the first year and lamented that our fast-paced culture typically does not. When all had spoken, the second and final spreading of Andy's ashes was conducted. Light, as they fell to feed the large roots of the redwoods.

SECOND ANNIVERSARY

The focus of my remarks at the second anniversary ritual was upon the themes of loss and attachment to which I have already alluded. A small group of friends and I were headed for Stanford to place flowers at Andy's tree and intended to share reflections before returning to Palmyra for a meal. Unfortunately, Carrie was traveling in Turkey at the time and was not present at the ritual. Even though I knew it was graduation weekend, I had not anticipated that this courtyard would actually be in use for a departmental degree ceremony. So, after having placed our flowers near Andy's memorial tree, we headed back up the hill to have the full anniversary among the redwoods as we had done the year before.

We were once again seated in the sacred circle of redwoods, where I shared my reflections. Others followed. Jeff, my new partner, was a psychologist I had met at a graduation party in the fall. We had spent significant time around my grief as we became better acquainted. Jeff had prepared his own reflections in advance, in the form of a letter to Andy and me:

Love Letter to Andy and the Father who
bears the face of his son.
June 17, 2001

My dear Andy,

Though I did not know you
You have revealed your essence and

have penetrated my life since October of last year when I met
your father,
deep into the Fall,
the continuing fall of your father's spirit—
Since then, and long before, the face of grief and the face of the
father have been intertwined.
You spoke to me in our remote and distant first meeting
at a celebratory gathering—a place I least expected to
find you, Andy—you, whose spirit had traveled so far
away.
A spirit heavy and laden with anguish, you were so far
away.
You coaxed me into a second meeting—my own years of deep
grief so ready to be re-opened.
You frightened me—your face of grief. Fearing that we would
fall into a well of sorrow irredeemable—you were confident
that we would manage.
I attended the first anniversary of your death in absentia—
reliving your loss through your father's reading of the talk he
gave that day.
I attended your tree planting—again, in absentia—further
agonizing sorrow-but you were present—in your fathers
heart, in the tears streaming down his face in the unendingly
anguished gulf between the world that was and the world
that is.
My deeper knowing of you, Andy, came when I attended
your funeral through a tape recording—ironically, it was
then that I came to know your person beyond the face
of grief.
I came to know your dutiful, reliable, and contained self—and
most importantly, your yearning for release—evident to everyone who spoke at the Stanford Chapel.

The face of grief that I have known as you, has now
been melded with the face of impermanence—the reminder
of all things passing and a confirmation of how short
time is.
This impermanence, like some people I have met in life,
seemed unnerving, harsh and frightening at first but, upon
closer acquaintance, proved to be far friendlier than I could
have imagined.

Your faces of grief and impermanence have become the legacies of your love.

To the unknown son I say:
I am grateful.

Washington Irving spoke about the sorrow we feel. He said:
"The sorrow for the dead is the only sorrow from which we refuse to be divorced. Every other wound we seek to heal, every other affliction to forget; but this wound we consider a duty to keep open; this affliction we cherish and brood over in solitude."

With the sorrow there is also a wish for you, Andy: That at this two year point you have safely made you way along the next leg of the journey—the transitions sometimes take awhile.

Love, Jeff

Clearly, Jeff was no stranger to grief, seeing the effects of death both in his personal journey as well as in his private practice. I concluded our circle by inviting all of us to talk during our meal about the attachments we had formed with one another over the years and their meanings. Ritual thrives on structure. By building in the expectation of focusing on the living attachments at the table, rather than depending upon pure spontaneity in which the exchanges I was hoping for might or might not occur, ritual allowed the personal to emerge. As we nurtured ourselves with food and heartfelt verses of our friendships, I was also given some unexpected grist for the mill. Both Carole and Dan, two of my best friends, reflected upon how difficult at times it had been for them to be around me and my intense grief these last two years. Dan's wording was something like: "*At times I just wanted to kick you in the ass to start letting go and feel life again.*"

All of them had recognized an upward shift in my energy since the spring, corresponding to having Jeff as a partner, and were relieved. I had not realized how hard this had been on my friends and feel very deep waves of gratitude that they did not retreat in the face of my suffering and measured out their attention to me with consistency during my mourning. In a culture so bankrupt in its own rituals around death, the individual commitment of those around us so often has to fill the void. And as they testified, this is no easy task. The lifting of the intensity of my grief was not only a consequence of time passing, as so many are too quick to assure the bereaved, but very much a result of the depths of relational energy from those who care about me.

ACT VI
Healing

I find it curious, but not surprising, that the portion of this book on healing is so short. Throughout the last several centuries, readers of Dante's *Inferno* and *Purgatorio* have far outnumbered those who have read his *Paradiso*. Apparently, suffering in the journey engages us more intensely than reaching the *gates*, beyond which our experience has not been as instructive. Folktales often begin with a state of deprivation—there is a famine, the King's daughter is without a prince, etc.—and the thrust of the plot is the unfolding of this dilemma and movement toward resolution. However, once the deprivation is met and a sense of balance returns (typified sometimes as *happily ever after),* there is no more story to be told. I have elicited from within myself a range of stories about my grief, but do not have as many to share about my healing. I recognize that I am still in the early stages of this healing, and more insights will emerge as I mature with the process. Also, I sense that the healing is more often the spaces between the words, *being* as it soothes, but not full of telling. At least, not yet. . . .

During that February night eighteen months into my grieving, which I have described in the *Despair* section, I turned to face the nothingness in my life. I felt my home was all that was there for me on a daily basis, and the challenge arose to offer it up. I did internally, not knowing what would be expected externally. The offering turned out to be symbolic rather than a spiritually *required* course of action. Paradoxically, Palmyra is now a focus for even more of my energies, and a vision I have for my daughter's future. What is required in the long journey toward healing is not always clear, logical, or orderly. Mystery, faith, and steps into the unknown are as much a part of grief's resolution as are knowledge, therapy, and research about how we mourn and heal.

Shortly before the third anniversary of Andy's death, a noticeable shift had occurred in my emotional valence toward this loss. When contemplating Andy's death, I was also able to entertain his life without overwhelming sorrow. Instead, I sometimes perceived opportunities to celebrate his humor, his respect for others, his insight, his beauty. The release of the darkness that occurred both at the funeral reception and the circle that followed at Palmyra, now had emerged more subtly, indirectly, and gradually. For the first time since Andy's funeral, on the third anniversary of his death, I displayed the photo boards depicting his two decades of life during our annual ritual. We laughed more about Andy and his foibles, taking him off the pedestal we mourners had built for him and allowing his human character to be jostled around a bit in our memories. Rather than ending our pre-meal ritual under the redwoods with the playing of Janet Jackson's "Together Again" with me sobbing away, I instead, throughout my remarks, played bits and pieces of five different versions of the song from the CD Andy owned. I gazed not only at the gathered friends, but up at the swaying tips of the trees that form the sacred circle as the remaining light of dusk funneled down.

Two factors, I surmised, were significantly responsible for such a transformation in the focus of my grieving. First, there was the catharsis that the writing of this book allowed. I had no intention of writing a book. But two months after the second anniversary of this death, I was walking back to my office on a pleasant August day and reflecting on the talk I had prepared for our gathering. By the time I was back in my office, the idea that there was a lot more to be shared and the intimidating vision of writing it all down was firmly in my consciousness. For years I have been teaching my students the following self-integration schema:

to recognize the presence of new internal impulses and thoughts

to name them once recognized

to dialogue with these newly named parts both within ourselves and also about them with trusted others

to accept them, even when they are dark

to act upon any insights that demand a response

to transcend, when possible, to new levels of awareness.

The die had been cast once I recognized the laborious but required challenge of writing out my grief. For, as in keeping a personal journal, writing down internal turmoil does not make it go away, but it has allowed me to take a step back from the intensity, even if momentarily. However, the dynamic nature of psycho-logical life required me again and again to check in with myself emotionally, for cathartic gains are rarely self-sustaining. So I wrote, rewrote, and dialogued endlessly with friends, hoping to write a clear story for others to hear, but not fully understanding how the process was healing me.

Secondly, a reviewer of the manuscript critiqued the work, as interpreting too much of the grief process as passive. He did, to his credit, disclose that he had never lost a child, and thus could not know from experience that such a blow can leave one so incapacitated that even breathing can be an accomplishment. But I heard his point, that even with terrible loss we need not remain fixed in pain. He stressed that we were capable of moving on with tutored lessons from our beloved. He wrote: "And there is also so much else that we continue to hold from those who have died, legacies, stories that have forever changed us and often for the better. Stories of their loves that are among the most precious we have ever learned, stories not canceled by death. And there are ways in which we can continue to feel their love for us and express our love for them, to love them in separation." Upon reading these words, I knew what he was referring to, for it was and is happening. I just had not recognized and named this part of the healing process so succinctly. The powerful capacity for empathy that grief teaches can be nurtured and sustained by the memories of and connections to the beloved. Andy, as son remembered, is spurring his dad on.

RELATIONSHIPS

The most dangerous time during my grieving was during the second autumn after Andy's dying, a few months into my year off from work. I was alone most days except for the few patients I saw in my private practice. My oldest friend in California and a fellow psychologist, Susan, had been keeping a close watch on me in her quiet manner since Andy's death. She knew that I was re-evaluating my career. She suggested during this fall that we form a small group of professional friends who were asking mid-life career questions and meet on a monthly basis. As the fall turned into winter, this monthly gathering of the four of us was the only human contact I had that was capable of staying with my pain, with the exception of my own weekly therapy. In psychological terms, it was a container that held the intensity of my grief for a couple of hours each month, even though our agenda was not solely focused on my grief. My introduction to Bill Bridges' book, *The Way of Transition*, and the valuable affirmation I received from its concept of the neutral zone, happened in the fourth session of this group.

In the week of Andy's death, one colleague had encouraged me to attend a group of parents who had lost children, but in that time of turmoil I had neither the focus nor the energy to find my way there. Susan's perceptiveness was on the mark both in the timing of her efforts to start such a group and the ease with which I could enter it, since it was composed of friends. She used the healing capacity of relationships in a carefully paced and patient manner to guard against my falling into a hole from which I might not have returned.

Another type of relationship also played a central role in my healing process. I met a friend about Andy's age, who had been diagnosed with brain tumors two years earlier and whose life expectancy was between four to eight years. We both were pretty needy fellows as we attempted to adjust to our new life circumstances and spent time hanging out together over many a game of pool with cynical humor between every other shot. Listening to a tape of David Sedaris' black humor about his mother's cancer diagnosis offered some cathartic laughter. Though others commented upon his obvious role as a substitute son, I assessed our dynamics more as partners in responding to the nasty hand life dealt us with the absurdity that we continue on each day for lack of a better plan. He went from a full head of thick young man's hair to baldness after starting radiation treatments, and his courage and savvy belief in his own self-importance was not only heartening to me, but was a check on my becoming too self-absorbed in grief. His present health has been amplified by his own intimate relationship, now a couple of years old, with a woman who has shown her own love by committing herself despite his medically predicted short life.

Tim, my contractor, played an important role during the second year of grief. I met Tim in one of the continuing education classes I had offered at Stanford several years before I purchased my home. After moving into Palmyra, there was some significant work that needed to be done to the structure. I was in the opportune situation to form a relationship with a contractor I so came to trust, that I never needed to have a firm estimate from him before any job. I asked him to help me build an additional shower during the fall of my year's leave. Coincidentally, his older brother had lost his very young daughter about the time of Andy's death, so Tim had been exposed to a parent in grief. Tim is the owner of a company that handles larger and upscale contracting jobs. However, he made time within his impossible schedule to both instruct me on putting up dry wall and similar tasks, and to take on parts of the project that were beyond my capacity. As we worked side-by-side he confronted my dark moods by consistently asking what good deed I had done for someone else recently. Since I was leaving Palmyra infrequently, I had little to report, but this did not dampen his inquiries. Finally I was able to share that I had written a letter to the parents of a high school senior that I read in the paper had been killed recently in an automobile accident. The energy to sit down, focus, and actually write such a letter was difficult to find in myself, but I knew Tim's reminders that I am part of a community of others who are in pain was on the mark. After two months of visits by Tim, I had my new shower and Tim submitted a bill noticeably below what his labor was worth. What he preached about good deeds, he had acted upon with me.

My friends Susan and Carole both revealed to me that a number of acquaintances had approached them to ask about my well-being through these last two years. The healing energy and spiritual protection that emerges when we hold others in our thoughts and prayers create effects I would be naïve and foolish to underestimate. Grief often isolates; relating heals. It heals both through the people that share our day-to-day living space, and those who may not be with us in place, but in spirit.

Over the last several years I have struggled with two contrasting observations about what we need as humans. Throughout the centuries, metaphysics has taught us that spiritual growth begins *inside,* that self-love is essential, that peace lies within ourselves. However, most psychotherapy practices are filled with people striving for love in their relationships. Social and medical sciences demonstrate, without a doubt, that we are inherently social creatures and do not thrive well if too isolated. I had been terribly lonely since the end of my marriage fifteen years before Andy's death. There had been two relationships, one a year and a half in duration, the second over four years, but no intimate relationship five years prior to Andy's death. I am self-conscious about the fact that I am not more settled or *existentially accomplished* at facing the aloneness. In humbler moments, though, I fully admit that I do need the love of another to support my spiritual growth inside of myself. Yet, I also shake my head as I realize that it is the intensity underlying this very longing for intimacy that so often seems to interfere with my being relaxed and patient when opportunities for love relationships are encountered. Grieving provides a microscopic view of loss and attachment, solitude and yearning for others. The relatedness in this grief process is so essential, even as I recognize that so much of the work can only be done alone.

The initial change in the daily intensity of my grief that February, a year and a half after Andy's death, was followed a few weeks later by the start of a new relationship with Jeff, which provided much-needed emotional support, social companionship, and sharing of intimacies. Jeff has said that he might not have approached me at the gathering where we met had I not revealed so much sadness in my non-verbal language. The intensity of my grieving also gave him pause—whether to go out on that first date after meeting, for entering into another's grief is a matter for *pause* and considerable discernment. One dimension of such an involvement is the continual awareness that all is ephemeral, and I can wake up one day being delivered news that my beloved has died, or has left. There is no way to wear armor and still love, yet I fear being plunged into more grief, so soon after losing my son.

I once again remember Andy's subtle response of empathy, as we left the tennis court the last day I saw him when I had made reference to my lonely heart. So unlike him. I imagine how pleased he is that his dad is now, for the present, less lonely. Had he been alive, he probably would have sought out a lot of involvement in my new relationship. But nonetheless, in his many silent moments, he would know how his dad was faring, for we have been attached since his birth. There will be neither a second family of kids from my new relationship, nor grandchildren from Andy's seed. And from my daughter . . . well, we shall see. Family, Carrie in particular, loyal and loving friends, and an intimate companion—all have played their roles well in this drama. It is a drama I would not have chosen them to be a part of, but, nonetheless, one which is as authentic as it gets. Alone, I do not believe I would have survived.

On a recent trip home to visit my elderly parents, my mother shared with me an experience she had the first Christmas after Andy's death. She was driving by herself several days before Christmas when a song came on the radio with lyrics about an angel looking down and reminding us humans of life's joys and assurance of protection. She suddenly felt that her angel grandson Andy was there for her and experienced a deep peace that had been missing since his death. She had neither heard this song before nor has heard it since but speaks with reverence of the *visitation* she experienced.

My mother possessed the intuitive wisdom to wait to share this story of healing until my own process was far enough along. Healing in one family member is not always a gift another can receive when grief is still far from resolved. As his grandmother and a woman of some seventy years, her healing came earlier. As his father, and a man of fewer years, my healing has been the marathon of my life journey.

CONCLUSION

I have just returned from a morning jog on the beach in Maui. I am here for a conference and have run each morning. I am surrounded and uplifted by the stunning beauty of the landscape, but I am also peaceful. However, such peace is never without an opposite tug for me: I feel sadness. I am melancholy pondering the world as I write: the desperation and fear motivating and resulting from acts of terror, impoverished people being bombed, the widening gap between the haves and have-nots. I feel particular empathy for those who have lost loved ones in these days of turmoil, knowing they face years of grieving ahead. The sadness is also more personal. This is my second visit to Maui, the first being in the late 1980s with Andy and Carrie. He was eleven, she thirteen, and we as a threesome were off on our first trip to the Islands. I did not think about that much as I arrived for this conference. Once on the beach, I see familiar landmarks. Memories emerge of those times shared with Carrie and Andy: sneaking into the resort swimming pools because we were staying at a modest condo a few miles off the beach; the ABC discount stores with their piles of tee-shirts; a sunrise trip to a volcano; and, of course, the Pacific, with its vastness and depths.

Remembering Andy here as a boy neither overwhelms me with intense crying today nor deprives me of being nurtured by time away on this island. These memories are like the flakes of filo in a Middle Eastern pastry, one's taste buds being engaged with the sweetness of the nuts and sugar, but the paper-thin dough also part of the mix. I will never be able to have a memory of him without missing him. But I have faced my grief, carried my grief, shared my grief, been angry about this grief, prayed to be able to bear such grief, written about this grief, and so the grief has offered some healing. Healing is not healed, all the energies of life within and without continue to dance in their cosmic yet highly personal steps, and I am, in this moment, without my son, for he has been released.

That which appears understandable, is not understood
All life includes death, which defines life
Death is always a passenger

POSTSCRIPT

Lane (1998, p. 122) writes: *I'm understandably reluctant to share the intimate story of my parents' deaths. Even though I know there's healing in the telling, especially in the kind of public telling that generally receives and expects no response. . . . I know also that there are rare occurrences in one's life when a window opens, when truth presents itself for a brief moment in all its stark intensity, and despite one's deepest reservations the resulting story simply insists on being told.*

I have told my story, as much a result of my own desire to move through this grief as to offer others who grieve a voice in their wilderness. So be it.

Resources

This list of resources is short because I have decided only to include material that I actually used and was helpful to me during the first two years of grieving. Friends recommended many books that I did not end up reading. I did begin several books but did not have the energy to pursue them to their end. There is, no doubt, a wide range of written and oral material that is crucial for those grieving. I am limiting myself here to mention those few which came my way, unsolicited, and which I leaned upon.

BOOKS

The Way of Transition: Embracing Life's Most Difficult Moments. William Bridges. Perseus Publishing, Cambridge, 2001.

Companion through Darkness: Inner Dialogues on Grief. Stephanie Ericsson. Harper Perennial, 1988.

Courtney's Legacy: A Father's Journey. George Cantor. Taylor Trade Publishing, Lanham, Maryland, 2001.

Lament for a Son. Nicholas Wolterstorff. William B. Eerdman's Publishing Company, Grand Rapids, Michigan, 1987.

MOVIES

The Son's Room. (2001) Italian.

Truly, Madly, Deeply. (1991) British.

MUSIC

Dance with Angels. 1999. Centaur.
(Includes Janet Jackson's "Together Again")

Keith Jarrett: The Köln Concert. 1975. BMG Classic.

ACTIVITIES

My exercise program, to be done for 80 years
Journal writing, including recording dreams
Prayer
Psychotherapy
Physical labor
Occasional massages
Crying during showers
Time with friends

References

Bridges, William. *The Way of Transition: Embracing Life's Most Difficult Moments*. Perseus Publishing, Cambridge, 2001.

Cantor, George. *Courtney's Legacy: A Father's Journey*. Taylor Trade Publishing, Lanham, Maryland, 2001.

Lane, Belden. *The Solace of Fierce Landscapes: Exploring Desert and Mountain Spirituality*. Oxford University Press, New York/Oxford, 1998.

Lewis, C. S. *A Grief Observed,* Harper & Row, San Francisco, 1989.

Miller, Arthur. *After the Fall*. The Viking Press, New York, 1964.

Sarton, May. As quoted in Lane, B. *The Solace of Fierce Landscapes: Exploring Desert and Mountain Spirituality*. Oxford University Press, New York/Oxford, 1998.

Weil, Simone, *The Path of Darkness*, quoted in Harper, p. 63. As quoted in Lane, B. *The Solace of Fierce Landscapes: Exploring Desert and Mountain Spirituality*. Oxford University Press, New York/Oxford, 1998.

Williamson, Marianne. Untitled. In *Life Prayers: Affirmations to Celebrate the Human Journey*. Edited by Roberts, E. & Amidon, E. Harper, San Francisco, 1996.

Index

Accidental Death and
    Dismemberment (AD&D)
    policies, 74–76
Activities, grieving, 110
Affection between father and
    son, 58–59
After the Fall (Miller), 50
Anger, 52–54
Anniversary rituals, 94–97,
    100
Announcement of the tragedy,
    7, 20
Ashes, spreading, 89–94
Attachment, the, 64–67
Attentiveness/inattentiveness
    and our own unconscious
    messages, 90–93

Banks, 70–72
Beebe, John, 89

Birthdays, 47
Birth story, 64
Buddhist perspective, 47

Car, the first, 59–60
Casket, open or closed, 25
Celebrations, death, 23
Circle, post-funeral sharing,
    34–37, 64
Collective trauma reactivating
    personal trauma, 62
Color, despair causing lost of,
    48
*Companion Through Darkness:
    Inner Dialogues on Grief*
    (Ericsson), 109
Contact, the need for, 21
*Courtney's Legacy: A Father's
    Journey* (Cantor), 22
Coworkers, 12–14
Crying, 45–47

Cultural customs around
mourning, differences in,
22–23, 32, 69

Dark journeys of the soul, 5
Despair after the rituals are
over, 47–52
Dreams, 19–20
Drino, Jerry, 32, 66, 69
Employer of deceased, 12–14
Eulogies at the funeral,
29–32
Existential level, anger at the,
53–54

Father-son dynamics, 54–55,
58–59, 91
Folktales, 99
Food given by sympathizers, 23
Forgetting, the, 60–62
Friends traveling distances to
be with survivors, 21–22
Frog Prince, 53
Funeral, the, 28–33
See also Post-funeral hours
Funeral industry, 8–9

Gifts from sympathizers, 23
Grandparents, 48, 49, 105,
106–107
Green, Maggie, 63
Green, Nicholas, 63
Green, Reg, 63

Healing process
inside, spiritual growth
begins, 104

[Healing process]
mystery/faith and steps into
the unknown, 100
peace tugging with sadness,
106
relationships, healing
capacity of, 102–105
spaces between the words, 99
writing, 100–101
Holidays, 47, 58
Home (physical building) as an
anchor during mourning,
51–52, 100
Hope under deep assault, 49,
50
Humor, cathartic, 102
Imperfections of the deceased,
55
Inattentiveness and our own
unconscious messages,
90–93
Inferno (Dante), 99
Insensitivity, unconscious,
52–53
Inside, spiritual growth begins,
104
Insurance, 74–76
Investigation of incident,
15–19
Isolation of grieving, 64–65,
88

Jackson, Janet, 56, 88, 100
Jewish ritual, 36–37
Jungian psychology, 20

Karpf, Jason, 31

Lament for a Son
(Wolterstorff), 109
Laramie Project, The (play),
47
Laughter, cathartic, 102
Legal system and
lawsuits/litigation,
78–86
Longing, the, 54–57, 106
Loss, phases in, 51–52
Loss coming without a chance
to respond/protect,
62–64

Marriage, death of child
affecting, 20, 27–28
Mediation and
lawsuits/litigation, 82–86
Memories, Dreams, Reflections
(Jung), 29
Memories triggered by life's
props, 57–60, 106
See also Stories about the
deceased
Minority group, those grieving
are their own, 70
Money, worries about, 8
See also Systems, bereaved
interacting with
bureaucratic
Music guiding through grief,
56, 88, 100, 110
Mystery and the healing
process, 100
Mystery and understanding,
33–34

Navajo Indians, 69
Neutral zone and phases in
loss, 51–52
Night after the death, the first,
11
Notification, death, 3–5

Paradiso (Dante), 99
Phases in loss, 51–52
Photographs, 40–43, 59
Physical work used to damper
despair, 48
Pieper, Joseph, 33–34
Planning the funeral, 9–10, 21
Police, the, 14–19
Post-funeral hours, 34–37,
64
Prayer, 35
Present moment, emptying
oneself into the, 63
Pride, parental, 55
Purgatorio (Dante), 99

Relationships, healing capacity
of, 21, 102–105
See also Ritual, sharing of
loss through
Remembering, the, 57–60
See also Stories about the
deceased
Repetitive expulsions of pain,
mourning and, 46–47
Resources, grieving,
109–110

Revenge, feelings of, 63
Ritual, sharing of loss through
    anniversary, second, 94–97
    ashes, spreading, 89–94
    circle, post-funeral sharing,
        34–37
    despair after the rituals are
        over, 47–52
    funeral, the, 28–33
    tree planting, 87–89
    wake, the, 24–28

Sabbatical taken to help
    recover, 47–48, 50
Scene of death, investigating
    the, 15–19
Sedaris, David, 102
Self-absorption, 69–70
Self-love, 104
September 11, 2001, tragedy of,
    62
Sermon, seeking person to say
    the, 10
Shame, feelings of, 5
Siblings of the deceased, 6–8,
    49
Silence, 21, 63, 99
Sioux Indians, 32
Society. See Systems, bereaved
    interacting with
    bureaucratic
Son's Room, The (film), 110
Spaces between the words,
    99
Stanford University, 9, 77–78
Stories about the deceased
    crying, 45–47

[Stories about the deceased]
    funeral, the, 29–32
    night after the death, the
        first, 11
    wake, the, 25–27
Support groups, 102
Synchronicity, 20
Systems, bereaved interacting
    with bureaucratic
    banks, 70–72
    insurance, 74–76
    legal system and
        lawsuits/litigation, 78–86
    overview, 70
    Stanford University, 77–78
    worker's compensation,
        72–74

Toddler, deceased as a, 59
"Together Again" (song), 56,
    88, 100
Tree planting ritual, 87–89
Truly, Madly, Deeply (film), 6,
    110

Unbearable Lightness of Being,
    The (Kundera), 90
Uncles, 48, 49
Unknown, healing process and
    steps into the, 100

Victim role for surviving
    parent, 69–70
Violence, grieving parents
    losing child through, 63

Wake, the, 24–28
Way of Transition, The: Embracing Life's Most Difficult Moments (Bridges), 50–51, 109
Weil, Simone, 63

Williamson, Marianne, 29
Worker's compensation, 72–74, 78
Worthington, Rossiter, 29
Writing helping the healing process, 100–101

About the Author

Douglas Daher, a psychologist at Stanford University, provides therapy for students at Vaden Health Center and teaches in the Psychology Department. His courses include: C. G. Jung and Analytical Psychology; Social Conflict and Models of Mediation; Human Sexuality; and Psychology of Religion and Inner Journeys: East and West. He has published numerous professional articles, written a series of modern folktales, and presented many papers at professional conferences. He co-developed the health-promotion board game *Sexploration* for college students. In addition to his work as a therapist, he supervises peer HIV testing counselors, participates on the Campus Sexual Assault Response and Recovery Team, and is consultant to university deans on psychological crises. He serves on the selection committee for the Andrew Daher Fellowship in the Haas Center for Public Service at Stanford, which provides grants for students to create economically-based projects for underprivileged communities. He was an All-American athlete in fencing at the University of Notre Dame and taught high school theology before returning to graduate studies. He now lives in Northern California among the redwoods.